RECOVERY FROM WITHIN

A MOTHER AND DAUGHTER'S JOURNEY THROUGH ANOREXIA

REBECCA PERKINS
BEATRICE ARSCOTT

To all those who are caught up in their thinking.

FOREWORD

We feel honoured to be sharing three forewords with you, each one quite different, each written by an expert in their field, each with a different perspective. We are immensely grateful to have Dr William Rhys Jones, Consultant Psychiatrist, Amy Johnson Ph.D and Mary Franklin Smith as our cheerleaders.

~

Eating disorders comprise a group of syndromes encompassing physical, psychological and social features and rank among the 10 leading causes of disability among young women. Anorexia Nervosa has the highest mortality rate of any mental disorder and affects about 1 in 250 women and 1 in 2000 men. About 5 times that number will suffer from Bulimia Nervosa which can be equally devastating for sufferers and their families. Recent research suggests that rates of eating disorders are on the rise however the evidence base for effective treatments remains frustratingly limited and the challenges of service provision mean that these treatments are not always available to people when they need it most. These ominous indicators have led clinicians, policy makers and researchers such as myself to explore how current evidence-based treatments can be delivered more effectively but has also highlighted the need to explore new ideas and approaches to treatment.

Although most people will have heard of eating disorders, the term 'eating disorder' is somewhat misleading as one could equally replace the word 'eating' with the word 'thinking', 'feeling', 'identity' or 'relationships'. The 'eating' side is often the part of the disorder which the world sees but underneath this veneer there lies a human being who is often lost in a sea of unhelpful thinking, existential uncertainty and loneliness. If left untreated this 'thought cloud' can grow in size, severity and pervasiveness such that it can feel and look like the eating disorder has taken over the person's very being. This doesn't have to be this way though and we know that treatment, particularly when given early on, can slow down or stop the 'snowball effect' and although many people go on to make a full recovery many sufferers often still report that they remain plagued by their 'anorexic thinking' which can lead to relapse and future difficulties. This suggests that perhaps our current approach to treatment, which aims to promote early behavioural change (e.g. increase in diet, reduction in excessive exercise) alongside psychosocial change, could be misguided or certainly could be enhanced by alternative theories or conceptual frameworks.

In Rebecca and Bea's book you will hear about their inspiring story and how they found the understanding they share about how the mind works to be ground-breaking in their journey. Although its evidence-base is very much in its infancy, the framework it provides in terms of conceptualising 'health' and 'thinking' has been extremely helpful and beneficial for countless people with and without mental health difficulties. Their story is one of many and these stories have inspired clinicians and researchers to explore how this understanding could potentially be utilised in a healthcare setting in the treatment of eating disorders and other mental health conditions.

Their story is one of hope, love and health and will no doubt strike a chord if you are experiencing similar challenges in your life or in the life of a loved one.

Dr William Rhys Jones is a Consultant Psychiatrist and Clinical Lead at CONNECT: The West Yorkshire and Harrogate Adult Eating Disorders Service, part of Leeds and York Partnership NHS Foundation Trust (LYPFT) and an elected member of the executive committee of the RCPsych Faculty of Eating Disorders. His research interests include early intervention in eating disorders, severe and enduring eating disorders, innate health, dual diagnosis and physical risk management in eating disorders. He is a media spokesperson for the Royal College of Psychiatrists and b-eat (the main UK based eating disorders charity) with recent appearances on BBC Breakfast and Panorama.

∽

The book you're about to read may look like a beautiful story about a mother and daughter's journey back to health.

It may look like a book about anorexia, or an inspirational book about the resilience of the human spirit, or the deep change possible with unconditional love.

It is all of those things, yet don't let it fool you. It is so much more than *just* those things.

Beneath the personal stories, the hope, and the inspiration are some profound truths about who we *all* are as human beings, each of the nearly eight billion of us on this planet experiencing life in our own flavor, with our own unique details.

When Bea was unwell, her unique details were often thoughts about food choices, weight, and nutritional content; feelings of fear, anger, and control, mixed with moments of gratitude and compassion and a million other passing, fleeting experiences.

Rebecca's details were more often slanted toward fear, despair and depression; combined with hope, overwhelming love for her children, and a million other passing, fleeting experiences.

Ever-changing, twisting, and turning throughout their journey, these details are what make the stories in this book so captivating and heartwarming.

But those details are not as deep or meaningful as they appear.

They say nothing about the true essence of Bea or Rebecca. Anorexia moved through Bea. Fear and depression moved through Rebecca. While Bea and Rebecca's details were unique to them in those moments, what lies *beyond* those details is universal and innate.

You'll know this is true because, as you'll read, their lives look very different today. Who they are was not tainted or damaged by those experiences, as difficult and traumatic as they were at the time. Who they truly are can't be touched by the comings and goings of thoughts and feelings.

Who they are — who we *all* are — is habit-free and fully well, by default, made of health and resilience.

Wellness is our true and unchangeable nature. The problem is that we mistake our experience — our fleeting, specific details — for who we really are. We mistake our struggles, our thoughts, feelings, desires, opinions, diagnoses, and fears for 'us'.

As Bea saw this more deeply, her eating-disordered thoughts began to look less stable and less real. She felt her health resurface, slowly but surely.

As Rebecca saw this more deeply, her despair and depression loosened their hold on her. She began to rediscover the peace and hope that had always been there within her.

This is the power and potential in the understanding Rebecca and Bea share. And it is true of all habits and all our issues, whether it's anorexia or panic attacks, bullying or insecurity, drinking, shopping, or working too much. The details are different for everyone, but the underlying truth is the same.

If there is one thing you take from this book, let it be a sense of that essence that is always there, unchangeable, within you as well. That spark of health and peace within. This is your solid place to rest no matter what specific experiences are coming your way.

These realizations led to deep change and a restoration of health for Bea and Rebecca. They live their lives connected to this health today. It led to deep change and a restoration of health for me too, from my own eating issues and anxiety, and for thousands of clients I've supported by sharing these truths.

I am so grateful you've found your way to this beautiful mother and daughter story, this journey back home for Bea and Rebecca. I urge you to look beyond the specifics and details of your own struggles to the universal truths to which they point. This can be the beginning of a journey back home for you, too.

Amy Johnson, Ph.D.

Author of *The Little Book of Big Change: The No-Willpower Approach to Breaking Any Habit*

~

During my work in a specialist NHS Eating Disorder service I have been witness to the devastating effects of anorexia nervosa on individuals and their families. I have seen how, in the stormy seas of anorexia, they toss and turn between moments of hopelessness, fear, isolation, courage, desperation, determination, worry, anxiety and exasperation. In this poignant and heartfelt sharing Rebecca and Bea will sit with you through this storm, explain it, recognise the pain and fear it causes, and point you to the calm beneath it. A calm that always has and always will be there.

If you're feeling isolated and believe that no one really understands where you are, then go ahead and turn the page... Rebecca and Bea have been where you are, they get it; you just have to look at the chapter titles to see that.

Recovery means different things to different people, but if

you seek a peaceful relationship with yourself and food then, with all of my heart, I would encourage you to look in the direction that Bea and Rebecca are pointing. Hope and love are woven throughout these pages and as Rebecca says "Hope is like love, it's expansive, it's creative, it's open, it's freeing."

Thank you darling Rebecca and Bea for this gift.

Mary Franklin-Smith, psychological, drama therapist and FREED champion, Leeds and York Partnership Foundation Trust.

ABOUT THE AUTHORS

We are Rebecca and Bea, mother and daughter, two human beings. It is a funny thing introducing yourself to someone who doesn't know you. Do we write a C.V.? What would you like to know about us? We looked at past biographies we'd written and this is what we decided to do instead...

We sat next to each other on the sofa, cups of tea beside us, laptops on our laps, and began writing about each other.

Let me introduce you to my daughter Bea:

This girl, this young woman who I am lucky enough to call my daughter, inspires me every day and I am so pleased to have her back from the grip of anorexia. If I am honest, for a while her nature, her kindness, love, courage, and determination, everything that makes Bea the woman she is, was hidden from view. There were times when I barely recognised her. There were times when I really struggled in our relationship. Now, things are so different. We have been on a journey and I feel enriched because of the love we have for each other. I am incredibly blessed to have such a close and loving relationship with her. It's a cliché, but we really have been there for each other, providing support through thick and thin, during the rough times and the great times. I like to think we have learned and taught each other how to embrace life fully. She teaches me about love and kindness. She teaches me about adversity and determination. She teaches me about courage and fear. She teaches me about fighting for something. She teaches me about pursuing something you believe in. She is the sort of young woman who inspires those around her; she always has time to listen to others; she cares deeply. She is generous, open-minded, and big-hearted. She is wise and thoughtful. If I were younger and her age I would want to hang out with her ... and I am honoured to call her my daughter.

Let me introduce you to my mum:

My mum is an incredible woman. She has dedicated so much of her life to raising me and my brothers so that we could become the best possible versions of ourselves. She always says her goal was to give us roots and wings — roots so we always knew where home was, and wings to be able to fly the nest and find our own way in life. This is something we have lived by, so much so that I now have it as a tattoo! Throughout my life, Mum has always been there for me, providing support and advice whenever I needed it. But it hasn't always been sunshine and roses. Our relationship has by no means been plain sailing. When I was unwell we shouted, yelled and cried. We slammed doors so hard they shook the house. I watched as she tiptoed on eggshells so as not to anger me. But having come out the other side (with a few metaphorical bumps and bruises) I feel extremely lucky that the hellish experience we went through has only brought us closer together. I gave her so much crap and yet she never left my side. She never gave up on me. She embodies the definition of true unconditional love, for which I am beyond grateful. I am so in awe of who she is and what she does that I would be proud to be half the mum that she is.

INTRODUCTION

"Everyone is doing the best they can, given the thinking they have that looks real to them."
~Sydney Banks

On New Year's Day 2008, our whole family was gathered together celebrating the end of one year and the beginning of a new one. We were seated around the dining room table enjoying a home cooked meal, raising glasses in celebration. But Bea's very observant cousin noticed that something wasn't quite right. He sensed that something was going on for Bea that no one else seemed to be aware of or, if they were aware, no one was talking about. After dinner (when Bea had left the room) he turned to his mum and asked her directly if she had anorexia. He had called out something Rebecca had started to become aware of, but had been desperately trying to ignore for many months. Bea was eating less and her portion sizes were becoming noticeably smaller. She was pushing food around her plate and had begun cutting out whole food groups entirely. She was exercising more and becoming more and more tired, lethargic and withdrawn.

Rebecca's sister broached the subject with her the next morning and Rebecca immediately felt sick. She knew. She'd guessed. And at the same time was ignoring it and willing it to go away.

No, really, this couldn't be happening to us, not anorexia.

A couple of weeks later we sat with the family doctor and listened as he confirmed what we already knew. Bea was diagnosed with anorexia nervosa. It sent shockwaves through the family and left us feeling both stunned and terrified. It was as if the road we were travelling on as a family had suddenly opened up in front of us and we had no idea what was about to unfold. What happens now? We felt such fear and uncertainty. We were launching into the unknown and it was utterly terrifying.

Over the months and years that followed, we battled with both the illness and each other to find a way through and out the other side. The last 10 years have been something of a rollercoaster, taking us to some frighteningly dark places. There were times when we weren't sure we'd make it and other times when we were filled with such hope.

Thankfully, and with enormous relief, we have come out the other side and have finally found a place of peace, wellbeing and recovery.

∽

Throughout this book we will share with you the insights we gained along the way and the understanding that has enabled us both to fully recover from the pain of anorexia. We have written the book we wish we'd had 10 years ago.

We first started talking about writing it several years ago when we were eager to share what we had been through, but at the time it all still felt too raw and without realising it, we still had a lot to learn. While Bea had been signed off by the doctors at this point, it wasn't until the end of 2017 that she has felt she has truly recovered. So, now feels like a good time to have put pen to paper.

~

This book is not a manual or a how-to guide about the dos and don'ts of 'treating' an eating disorder. Neither is it a memoir. It is not the story of Bea's day-to-day battle with eating. It is not an account of Rebecca's struggles caring for her daughter, although you will certainly read about some personal stories within the book that bring our story to life.

What we felt was more important to write about are the keys to unlocking your own recovery. And right now that might sound utterly crazy to you, the notion that you can unlock your own recovery. We know this to be true and want to share what we have learned and seen in Bea's healing and recovery.

In 2016 we came across a new understanding of how the mind works that changed everything. We have decided not to share and explain it here in the introduction because the details of it are not as important as the implications it has had for Bea's healing and recovery. We have devoted an entire section to the understanding, known as The Three

Principles, towards the end of the book. Take a look at Section 5 entitled 'Innate Wellbeing'.

What we do want to share with you now is what we have come to understand about our experience of day-to-day life. We also want to show you the transformational impact this understanding can have. Because of this, Bea has been able to free herself completely from the eating disorder that had been with her in the shadows for over a decade.

Two themes particularly stand out for us:

We all have innate mental wellbeing

By this we mean that by our very nature we are all mentally well. Innate means that this is who we are; it is our default, factory setting. We all have access to this innate wellbeing - it's what we're born with. The only thing that keeps us from it is our thinking. Peace of mind, clarity, wellbeing is who we are; it is truly our natural state. Every human being has the capacity for wellbeing. Knowing that changes everything, for everyone.

Let us explain it using a simple metaphor. The sky is always blue, even behind the darkest clouds and the wildest weather. We know that once the weather passes we will once again see the blue sky. We never doubt this, we don't question it, even if we've not seen blue sky for days. We don't panic or try to fix the weather; we know that we simply have to sit it out, keep dry or out of the wind and someday soon the blue sky will return.

We are the same, exactly the same. We are the blue sky. Our natural state is one of mental health, wisdom, resilience and clarity. We do not have to be defined by the internal weather that passes through us. Sometimes that weather looks like stress, depression, addiction, an eating disorder, lack of confidence or panic attacks. It is not who we are. It is *never* who we are. We are all okay and well at a very basic and fundamental level. It is only ever our thinking that gets in the way of us seeing this and knowing it to be true. Whatever you are believing about yourself right now that is keeping you from innate wellbeing does not need to define who you are. For a long time Bea felt that anorexia defined her identity, because that's all she could see. But she now knows that it doesn't have to be that way and that our mind will always return to its default state if we allow it.

We are all okay. All of us. Whatever our 'condition'. This is what we saw. Realising this and taking it to heart, rather than simply understanding it intellectually, is what enabled Bea to fully recover. We know the same is possible for you.

Here's the second thing we saw:

We only ever experience life from the inside out

Let us explain what we mean by this because that sentence may make no sense to you. What we mean is, the way we feel is not actually a direct result of our circumstances, our situation in life, or the people around us. On the surface it certainly looks this way, and until a couple of years ago it was something we believed and didn't even question. Yet we've learned that this is just not true.

Look at it this way. A piece of cake can't make you feel happy or sad; it's cake. It just doesn't have that kind of power. Sometimes it really feels like it does though. What's actually happening is that external circumstances — relationships, jobs, the weather, cake — trigger our brains to create thoughts. Our brilliant minds then instantly turn these thoughts into feelings and hey presto we feel something (and sometimes that feeling can be quite extreme). We feel stress or delight or nothing at all towards the cake. The thing is, it's not the cake that's making us feel this way, it's our thinking. Two people could stand in front of the same piece of cake and experience completely different feelings towards it.

Here's another example. When Bea was unwell it really felt like the numbers on the bathroom scales were causing her to feel upset, angry, anxious or happy (depending on which way the numbers were going). Yet the numbers on the scales didn't cause those same feelings in Rebecca. She didn't really have any thinking about the scales at all. So, if that's the case then what was causing emotion in Bea wasn't the bathroom scales themselves but her own personal thinking about them and what she had decided the numbers meant.

What this shows us is that it's only ever what we *think* about what's happening around us that influences how we feel. In other words, we are always living in the feeling of our thinking. However, we've always being told that it works the other way — that a new car will make us happy; that the latest face cream will make us feel 10 years younger. Society is set up this way; we see the outside world as the thing that's altering our state of mind — it's the government, it's our boss, it's the traffic, it's our partner.

Gradually, over time, we both started to notice where we had believed this to be true in life. But instead of taking it as fact, we started to question whether, actually, we had got it all wrong. When we both understood that life only works from the inside out, everything seemed to fall into place. We saw how this could impact all areas of our lives and realised that this truly was the key to alleviating all our suffering.

But so what? What does this actually mean in practice? We're not trying to say that we now never get anxious, stressed, or upset. That certainly isn't true! Yet by knowing that our thoughts, rather than those external factors, create our feelings we can:

- Take the thinking we have a little less seriously
- Question beliefs and stories we have bought into about ourselves and others
- Better understand why people act or behave in a certain way

To us, the implications of this understanding of how the mind works were incredible. Bea had come to accept that she would always be 'living with anorexia', but this is thankfully no longer the case. Anorexia is no longer an issue in Bea's life and she has fully recovered.

We hope you find something in this book that will help you or your loved one to see that full recovery really is within reach.

Read on because we've got a lot to share ...

What we will cover in this book

The book will cover five key themes, which we hope will resonate with you whether you currently have an eating disorder or are caring for someone who does. At the end of the book we also share our hopes for the future. The themes we will cover are:

- Thoughts and Beliefs
- Feelings and Emotions
- Identity
- Relationships
- Innate Wellbeing

Within each of these sections we have written a number of short chapters, some written by Rebecca, some written by Bea. Feel free to open the book anywhere and start reading or see which chapters appeal most to you. There is no right or wrong way to read the book. Start wherever makes sense to you.

Throughout the book we will be sharing the insights that changed how we understand eating disorders and how it really is possible to achieve complete recovery.

We are so glad that our book has found its way into your hands.

Notes

- Sometimes it might sound like we are repeating ourselves. This is done deliberately. Often we don't hear things the first time around. Sometimes we can understand a concept intellectually but it's not until we understand it at a deeper level that we truly see it
- We suggest that you take your time reading this book. Read to get a sense of what we're saying rather than reading it as a textbook or a book you have to analyse. In other words, pay more attention to how you feel rather than what you're thinking about whilst you read. When we go to the cinema

we sit and watch, we take it all in rather than sitting as a film critic. We get an overall sense of the film, and our focus is more on how it makes us feel.

- We'll be sharing a simple understanding that might on the surface look too good to be true. We get that. Hang in there.

This is a story of hope and one we wish to share with mothers and fathers, sons and daughters, brothers and sisters, grandparents, aunts and uncles, boyfriends, girlfriends, friends, and anyone in the grip of an eating disorder.

Together we survived the toughest experience of our lives and are now thriving. We want this book to offer support and guide those suffering with an eating disorder to their own recovery.

With our love,

Rebecca and Bea x

September 2018

SECTION 1: THOUGHTS AND BELIEFS

*"All you have to know is everything is created from Thought, you
don't have to know anything else."*
~ Sydney Banks

Understanding thought was the piece of the puzzle that was
missing for us for a long time. What we want to share with
you in this section of the book is just how incredible the
power of thought is in creating our experience of life.

Rebecca sat in a conference recently listening to speakers
share both the simplicity of this understanding (referred to
by Sydney Banks as The Three Principles), and the far
reaching implications for us as human beings. She heard
one speaker say that the human mind is able to heal all by
itself once it has an understanding of the role that thought
plays in our experience. It was true. We'd seen it for
ourselves many times. Thought really was creating our
experience of life. Indeed, thought is creating the life that
you're experiencing right now.

However, it often looks like our experience is coming from

circumstances around us, from people, our situations, and where we find ourselves in life. To be honest, there are still days that it looks that way, yet we now know that it's only ever coming from within us. Our personal thinking creates our world.

Until we see this for ourselves we risk being the victims in our own lives because we're totally at the mercy of circumstances, people and our situation. When we see it as it really is we can no longer be the victim.

We live in the feeling of our thinking. We have a thought, which in turn creates a feeling — a good feeling, an unpleasant feeling, or a neutral feeling. We often get scared of our feelings. We resist and we end up feeling tense, anxious, or depressed. We believe we have to change our thinking. Rebecca spent years trying to do this (which was all done in good faith, she'd read a ton of books on it!) We believe we have to stop our thinking, that we should get to a place of 'no thinking'. This isn't what we're saying.

Whilst you read this section consider these three things:

- The transient nature of thought — the way they come and go without any effort
- Notice what happens when you begin to pay less attention to your thinking
- Consider how much of what's going on in your head is actually true

1

WHY I NO LONGER FEAR FOOD

BEA

Having anorexia wasn't a deliberate choice. It wasn't 'extreme dieting gone wrong'. For some reason, subconsciously and very quietly, a voice in my head just started telling me that food was no longer my friend—that fat, carbohydrates, and any sort of 'fun' foods were simply off limits.

To this day I don't know what caused it. It could have been any number of things, but to be honest, not knowing doesn't really matter to me. What I see now is that I believed a series of thoughts and stories that, at the time, seemed to make sense to me. Stories about what I could or couldn't do; thoughts about what I should or shouldn't eat.

One of the things I did (again, completely subconsciously) was to create what I called my 'blacklist'. This was a list of foods that I saw as no-goes: fried foods, red meat, creamy sauces, cake, pizza, cheese, pasta, the list goes on...

These were the sorts of foods that I would choose to never,

under any circumstances, eat. And if, for whatever horrendous reason, I was forced to eat something from this list, I would often feel physically sick just at the thought of doing so.

I would even feel a physical sensation, an uncomfortable tingling all over my body, when I ate those foods. It was like I could feel the food clinging to my skin.

While now I'm able to reflect back and see this list for what it really was — a figment of my imagination — at the time, it was my reality, it was my bible. And until relatively recently, almost ten years after my original diagnosis, it felt so real that I'd never questioned its existence.

Going out to restaurants was always a torturous occasion. All menus had to go through a thorough vetting process before a restaurant was chosen so I could make sure it was 'safe'. Predictability was so important to me. Routine meant that there was less thinking and decision making required. It removed the uncertainty. If I was ever presented with a different brand of food than what I was used to, it would totally throw me. I knew exactly how many calories were in each of my 'safe' foods at home. Any deviation from that would completely unsettle me.

I kept my blacklist alive for 10 years. I didn't know that I didn't have to. The restrictions I put on my diet felt so normal that I never thought to question what I was doing. But then a friend challenged me on my list and gently woke me up to the fact that actually I could choose. I could choose not to believe the thinking that was telling me that I couldn't eat what was on that list. She helped me realise that my list was make-believe, and I didn't need it to keep me safe.

Over the weeks following that conversation the list just seemed to fade away. Putting those restrictions on myself suddenly didn't seem to make sense anymore. It really was as simple as that. There was no effort involved. I didn't have to *try*. All that happened was that I saw something from a different perspective. It's a bit like when you're young and afraid of the dark. At some point, for no particular reason, you just stop being afraid. It no longer makes sense.

So that's what happened to my blacklist. I'm not suggesting that I'm now scoffing KFC family buckets any chance I get. I'm still health-conscious, making healthy, nutritious meals for myself and others, but that's just how I was brought up. What this realisation has meant is that I'm now able to rediscover the foods that I had put off limits for all those years. It has meant that I can decide for myself whether or not I like them.

And this rediscovery is still happening. Just the other day I was at a restaurant and automatically looked for the salad section on the menu. Over the last 10 years I had trained myself to not even look at the other options — to me they were off limits. But I suddenly remembered that I can eat *anything* I want. I let myself enjoy browsing the entire menu and picked something that I actually wanted to eat.

Self-judgment is something I had become pretty good at over the years. Previously, if I had eaten something that I had deemed to be off limits, I would have spent so much time and energy punishing and judging myself for doing so. But I don't have to do that anymore. I never *had* to in the first place, it just seemed like the most logical thing to do at the time. I'm now giving myself permission to enjoy food and the experiences that come with it.

What I find so interesting about this is that it's all about storytelling. I was telling myself a very compelling story that I wholeheartedly believed: "If you eat that pizza you're going to feel sick and uncomfortable. You're going to get fat and that's not what's going to make you happy is it?!"

Crazy, right?

But once we are able to see these stories for what they are — thoughts that we believe to be true — we don't have to pay them any attention. We can stop believing them. We really do have that choice.

Despite what your English teacher may have told you at school, it turns out that we're all pretty convincing story-tellers. And while this can sometimes be helpful, often we are unintentionally holding ourselves back: "I'm too young to get that promotion", "I'm not good enough to write a book", "I'm not brave enough to eat that". You get the idea.

But no matter how convincing that story may be, you don't have to believe it. Really, you don't. And when you realise that, it can be pretty liberating.

Sometimes those stories are not always easy to spot, particularly if we've believed them for some time. They can become so ingrained in everyday life that we just don't think anything of them. That was certainly the case for my black-list. But when I do notice them, I ask myself: "How much of what I'm thinking right now is actually true?" And more often than not, the answer is, "not a whole lot". It allows you to see through things that you had previously taken to be "fact". It also makes you realise how much we limit ourselves in life and how many opportunities and possibilities are open to us once we understand that it's our own thinking that is creating our experience.

2

NO FIXING REQUIRED, NOTHING IS BROKEN

REBECCA

I've been thinking back to a time when I was stuck in my thinking, it was at a time when I was plagued with depression. I really thought there was something wrong with me. There were days that I really believed I was broken. I questioned why this was happening to me, what had caused it, would I ever feel better and brighter again, how would I cope raising my three children in this negative state of mind. I looked outside for something to fix me. I spent a lot of money on every self-help book I could lay my hands on and saw a number of therapists. I felt hopeless.

So many of us feel lost at different times in our lives and because we believe that our experience of life comes from 'outside' we look for signs to prove that we're broken, or inadequate or lacking in some way. We find evidence everywhere we look to prove this to ourselves. This reinforces our feelings of inadequacy, and of brokenness. I remember one time when I was suffering with depression, I needed to get a birthday card sent off to a friend. I'd bought the card, but writing it and putting it in an envelope, buying a stamp and sending it off in the post felt like scaling Everest for me. It took me several weeks — a clear sign of my 'brokenness' in my mind at the time.

Having spoken with Bea, this is certainly something that she felt. She had a diagnosis that was a sure sign that something was wrong with her in her eyes. The diagnosis prevented her from doing certain things. Her rowing coach and I had made the decision together to stop allowing her to be part of the squad because her weight wasn't acceptable given the intensity of the training. We'd arranged that Bea would eat her school lunch in the nurse's office. All these decisions — whether right or wrong — were pointing her towards the 'fact' that she was in need of help.

And yet, I never really saw her as broken. Perhaps that's a mother's desire to always see the best in her child. I suspect it was something more profound in that I knew somewhere in the recesses of my mind that she, like everyone else on the planet, can never be broken. We are created whole, there is nothing that needs fixing, we are never broken. The only thing that separates us from our wellbeing is our belief in our thinking. That's it.

I know that sounds overly simplistic.

The moment we understand that we aren't defined by our thinking, then so much of what we've believed and held close all these years simply begins to fall away. We don't need to take our thinking so seriously.

I appreciate that this might make no sense to you right now. All I ask is that you don't discount what we're saying, stay open to hearing something that you've not heard before.

You'll be hearing both Bea and I say that certain thinking no longer made sense anymore. And that's exactly what it was like. Beliefs we'd both held for years, decades in my case, just fell away. Wellbeing is always present; it is only what we do with our thinking that leads us to feelings of lack or being limited in some way. It is through thought that we create either heaven or hell for ourselves.

As I'm writing this I've got my own questions coming to the surface, actually questions that you may well be asking about the whole notion of 'nothing's broken or needs fixing'. You may well feel that your life or the life of someone you love and care for deeply looks broken; you might even say that it is broken. And what right do I have to tell you otherwise... I get that.

Here's what Bea and I see. Beneath all the noise, beneath all the fear, is a place of wellbeing. Strip everything back to the essence of who we are and you'll find that we are all okay.

3

CAUGHT UP IN MY THINKING

BEA

I have a confession to make.

I don't remember a huge amount from the time when I was suffering with anorexia. Certain things I can remember as if they happened yesterday. I remember the things I used to do to avoid eating, like hiding snacks down the side of the sofa and pouring drinks away when no one was looking. I remember the feeling of pride and terror when I hit my lowest weight.

I remember going to the hospital. I remember turning down a biscuit the doctor offered to me when I felt faint during a weigh-in. I remember drinking several bottles of water before my weigh-ins to add on extra weight. However, I also remember the huge sense of pride I felt after eating the corner of a chocolate brownie on my 16th birthday.

But for some reason, I have very few memories from around that time that are not about food. I don't remember much about school. I have very few memories of social events. I don't even remember much about my family and friends during that time. I have recollections of my older brother, Ollie, being hugely protective of me as older brothers are, but specific memories seem just beyond my reach.

I've found this gap in my memory hugely frustrating, particularly when we started talking about what we would write about in this book. It's part of the reason why I didn't want to start writing it sooner. I couldn't understand why these memories had vanished. Why could I remember certain things so clearly and have so many gaps elsewhere?

But then the answer suddenly became clear to me. I realised that my inability to recall memories from that time isn't because I knocked my head or developed amnesia. I came to the conclusion that it must be because during that time I was so stuck in my own head, getting tangled up in my thinking, that I wasn't paying attention to anything that wasn't related to food or my eating disorder. I can't remember anything because, mentally, I wasn't giving it enough attention to log it in my memory.

We all get caught up in our thinking from time to time. Whether it's going back over a conversation you had earlier that day or worrying about how you're going to pay for a new boiler, we all do it. When I was suffering with anorexia, I was in a constant state of being caught up in my thinking.

My whole world revolved around food and my eating disorder. It was all I ever thought about. It occupied every corner of my consciousness. From the moment I woke up in the morning to the moment I slumped back into bed, I was thinking about what I was (or wasn't) going to have to eat that day or the next. I was fantasising about what I would eat if I didn't have anorexia. I was thinking about how much I hated going for my weigh-ins at the hospital and how no one understood how I was feeling. It was constant and it was exhausting.

But what I didn't realise at the time was that above the thunderstorm of thought that was constantly raging, there was blue sky — a place of peace and quiet. To use the metaphor we used in the introduction, I didn't realise that blue sky is our default setting. No matter what thoughts come and go and no matter how long they may linger, they will pass and our minds will clear.

There were moments during the time that I was unwell when the clouds would clear and I would realise that I did want to get better. But then another cloud would come along and I'd be back in the loop of unhelpful thinking.

Over the years that I suffered with anorexia, I became so engulfed by my thought storms that I didn't actually realise they were made from thought and that they weren't real. The voice in my head telling me not to eat was so loud and so persuasive that I couldn't see it for what it was — an illusion. The dictionary defines an 'illusion' as: "something that deceives by producing a false or misleading impression of reality." I was creating an incredibly convincing one, but I can now see that that's what it was.

At the time, my thinking was telling me that eating was a bad thing. It was telling me that I wasn't thin enough, despite having a Body Mass Index (BMI) that told a different story. And it felt completely real, which is why I didn't question it. But the more attention you give to a particular thought, the more convincing it looks and feels because the mind has to come up with new, convincing reasons for you to continue buying into it. It's a bit like a lawyer in a court of law bringing out more evidence to back up their argument.

But if you can shine a light on the illusion to expose the fact that there's no substance, no truth to it, you can start to take it a bit less seriously.

I was doing the best I could with the thinking I had at that time. To me, restricting my eating seemed like the best thing to do, because that's what the thoughts in my head were telling me. But I didn't know back then that I could question them. I didn't know that the stories that were being created in my head weren't always true. So, with that understanding, I was doing the best I could. And that's all we're ever doing in life. If I'm in a crappy mood, I'm having crappy thinking. But in that moment, whatever I'm doing, I'm still doing the best I can with the thinking I have. Knowing this enables us to be more understanding and empathetic when others are behaving in a certain way. It also gives us licence to cut ourselves some slack.

4

I DIDN'T REALISE I COULD IGNORE MY THINKING

REBECCA

There was a time not that long ago that I believed all my thinking. Well, it was in my head so it must be mine and therefore true. I didn't question it. Ever. Whose was it if it wasn't mine? If you'd have asked me, I'd have said that I believed everything I 'heard' in my head. I know I'm not alone! Bearing in mind that we have around 60,000 thoughts a day it was pretty noisy in there. Hardly surprising therefore that I felt exhausted much of the time.

There was a whole gang of voices arguing, debating, yelling, cajoling, urging, whining, pleading, cheerleading, quizzing, wondering.

And then what about all those feelings? In any one day I could feel joy, depression, guilt, anger, frustration, pride, hopelessness, amusement, envy, helplessness, peace, and worry. What was I meant to do with them all?

It's possible to lurch quickly and randomly between feelings of sadness and joy, loneliness and peace, feelings of regret and relief. I can be sobbing one minute and the next it's gone. Just think of a baby or a toddler and you'll understand the fleeting nature of thought and feelings. They hang on to nothing. They lurch through a whole selection of moods at any one time, easily moving through rage to laughter in a moment. What a great lesson for us grown-ups!

Most days it felt like I was carrying around an overstuffed bag on my back. I lived with sciatica and lower back pain. Lugging all those thoughts and feelings around all day long was tough business and it was causing real physical pain.

And then the light bulb moment. Following a lifetime of searching and signing up to class after class to find some kind of peace of mind, here it was, right under my nose.

"Thought is not reality, yet it is through thought that our realities are created."
~ Sydney Banks

That's it. I saw it.

My personal thinking is being brought to life via the very fact that I am conscious, which is literally turning every 'neutral' thought into a hi-definition, surround-sound movie right in front of my eyes.

I realised that I was creating anything from a horror movie to a romcom, from an awesome documentary to a spy thriller all day long. It had nothing to do with the world out there! It was all my creation. None of it was real. None of it was true. But boy did it look that way.

And here's one of the greatest things I learned — thought is transient. It's fleeting, it's like clouds passing in the sky, just as they are outside my window right now. When we don't get involved in the detail of our thoughts, they pass. We can let them be. There is nothing we need to do.

There was absolutely no need for me to be carrying around this ludicrously heavy backpack. I could simply take it off by not taking my thinking so seriously.

One day I did indeed put down the rucksack. It no longer made sense to carry it around. Just as Bea mentioned in the previous chapter, there was no effort involved, I just stopped taking my thinking so seriously. Oh, there are some days I find myself drawn to picking it up again and believing all of those unhelpful stories about myself. But as I find myself feeling its weight (and it's always a feeling that gives me a clue) I am able to put it down again. Putting it down, seeing through the illusion of thought, restores me to my quiet mind and from that place I have peace and clarity and a deeper love and understanding of life.

At times when Bea was ill I found myself believing a lot of my thoughts. At times I believed that it was my fault that she was ill. I searched for things I might have done or reasons that suggested how I'd parented had caused her to suffer. Perhaps my love felt claustrophobic? Perhaps my love of food and cooking had had a detrimental effect. I could spend hours wading through thoughts in order to try to make sense of why Bea was suffering.

I now see that all of this was made up. I simply didn't have to believe my thinking.

5

OBSESSING OVER NUMBERS

BEA

When I had anorexia, life was all about numbers. How many calories was I eating? How many was I burning off? How many kilograms did I weigh? What size jeans was I wearing?

When it came to eating, it was a numbers game and I was constantly challenging myself to see how low I could go (without getting caught, of course). And this would dictate how I felt. The lower the numbers (calories, fat content, sugar etc.) went, the greater the sense of satisfaction and achievement I felt. The higher the numbers, however, the worse I felt. If I consumed "too many" I would fly into a spiral of self-hatred, resentment and anger. I would feel physically sick, not because I was full, but because I was so repulsed by what I had done.

Throughout this period in my life, I assigned so much importance and meaning to numbers. They completely controlled what and how much I ate. If an item of food exceeded my made-up daily calorie limit then it became a no-go. It was added to my blacklist.

The amount of attention I gave to the numerical value of different foods meant that over time I built up a wealth of knowledge of the calorie content of the foods I ate. I knew how they varied between different brands of sliced bread, for example. I knew how many were contained in the individually flavoured yogurts in the variety pack Mum would buy for me. On the plus side, my mental arithmetic significantly improved as I totted up the figures throughout the day!

Thinking back now, I find it ironic that at school I was hopeless at remembering statistics or dates, and yet I became an expert at memorising the calorie content of pretty much any food with which I came into contact. In History lessons I could never remember significant historical dates. In Geography I would always forget how many people had been impacted by a particular earthquake or indeed the year it happened. Numbers just didn't seem to stick when they weren't part of my anorexia world.

But those that *were* part of my world soon came to define me. When I went to the hospital for my weekly weigh-ins, I was judged (and I in turn judged myself) on whether my weight had gone up or down. I soon became equally as obsessed with the numbers that looked back at me on the weighing scales as I did with the food I put in my body. To me these numbers were an illustration of how well I was doing at being anorexic. As with food, the lower the number, the more successful I felt.

While I had taken it to the extreme, the meaning and importance we assign to numbers in everyday life is not unique to people with eating disorders. Nicola Bird (https://alittlepeaceofmind.co.uk/) sums this up really well in her blog, 'A life of arbitrary numbers'.

The fact is, we all do it and we use it as a measure of success or failure: "I'll be comfortable when I have £X in the bank, but anything below that means I need to worry". "I'll be happy when I weigh Ykg, but any heavier means I have no self-control". "I'm a good daughter if I call my mum Z times a week, but any fewer means I'm not". I don't think we realise how much meaning we give to numbers on a day-to-day basis and, when you think about it, how arbitrary they really are. I don't think we even realise that the numbers are there in the first place.

But once you notice that you're playing out your life within these fictitious boundaries, you can realise that they're all made up and you don't need to pay them so much attention. When I'm looking at what to buy for my lunch and I automatically reach for the sandwich with the fewest calories because I feel I *have* to, I can ask myself the question: "Says who?"

The other day I was in this exact situation. I was in the queue at the supermarket, bland sandwich in hand, when I suddenly realised that I could switch off my autopilot thinking and actually choose something delicious. I left the queue and picked up one of those posh sandwiches with the fancy packaging: Wiltshire ham, mature cheddar, and pickle. It was my first cheese sandwich in almost 15 years. But instead of worrying about the numbers on the front of the packet, I gave my overthinking mind some time off and just enjoyed it. I won't lie, I did have a moment of insecurity when I looked at the calorie content, but then remembered that it was my thinking, rather than the numbers, that was making me worry. I remembered that I could allow myself to enjoy it without worrying.

Anyway, I did eat it, I did enjoy it, and I am still alive.

I can now see how numbers, whatever they refer to, can't *make* me feel anything. I can add meaning to them which in turn can cause me to feel a certain way, but on their own they have no power. Simply noticing that we've made it all up gives us permission to let go, which, from experience, opens us up to a whole world of new experiences.

IN SEARCH OF A QUIET MIND

REBECCA

Freedom from an eating disorder, or anxiety, or OCD, or whatever consumes our minds and weighs down our thinking is what we're all searching for. With the benefit of hindsight and an understanding of how the mind works, Bea and I found this place to be in a quiet mind.

If I was to tell you that there are no tools or strategies or willpower tactics or anything that requires any effort, you'd most likely want to tell us that we just don't understand. You may well believe that you don't have that capability, you just don't have that space where it's quiet inside, you just don't have access to a quiet mind.

I'd encourage you to hang in there; we see things when we're ready to see them. Pushing to try to see something or hear something takes us further away from the answer. I know that, because I've tried it many times.

This is true everywhere. You may well be struggling to make sense of what we're sharing right now. You may be caught up in even more thinking. It's okay. We were the same too.

Let me share a story with you.

I spent a week in Edinburgh during the festival in August. I was walking with my friend through the Chinese Hillside within the Botanic Gardens. We stood on the bridge looking into a vast pond filled with water lily leaves. We'd been talking about life and, more specifically, where our experience of it comes from. Some of the leaves were vivid green and some were faded and yellowing. I asked my friend whether there were ever any water lilies or was it just leaves that filled the pond. And then suddenly, literally out of what seemed like nowhere, I saw the lilies — they were yellow and the pond was filled with them, all bursting into bloom. And now when I looked all I could see were the flowers sitting on the leaves. I could no longer not see them!

How was it, we wondered, that just moments before neither of us could see the flowers. They were clearly there, we just couldn't see them. This led us into a beautiful conversation about our own blind spots in life.

Until 2016 I believed that my experience of life came from my circumstances, the things happening around me, outside of me, and via the people in my life.

- I believed that someone really could make me feel a certain way, whether that was angry or happy or any emotion in between
- It really seemed as if the weather could affect my mood
- I thought my happiness came from regularly receiving texts from my children

- It appeared that my happiness was dependent on my children, my family and my friends
- I believed if I was the perfect parent I'd feel happy

These were some of my blind spots.

And, as suddenly as I saw the water lilies on the pond, in the same way and just as quickly, I saw that my wellbeing, my experience of life only ever came from inside me. My experience of life was being created via my thinking moment by moment.

I saw that nobody can actually make me feel anything, even though it really feels like that at times. I realised that I'm only ever reacting to my thinking about that person, in that moment.

I saw that the weather can never affect my mood, even though when it's pouring with rain again, it can often look that way! I just have to remember the times when it has been really sunny and I've felt miserable or when there's a wild storm and I've felt on top of the world.

It's never the weather. It's always my thinking.

I began to see that my feelings were simply my internal barometer, informing me of what my thinking was up to.

A low feeling was simply telling me that my thinking was probably not reliable; it wasn't a trustworthy gauge of anything important. A good feeling, on the other hand, was telling me that my thinking was worth trusting. For example, when Bea was ill and I felt deeply frustrated, because this was all so new to me, it would have been good to know that letting go of that thinking would have led to a quiet mind. From this place I would have been likely to come up with thinking and solutions that were more helpful.

When I was a child I used to love watching my dad gently tap the barometer in the hallway of our home to see what was happening to the weather. Was low pressure on its way in or was high pressure on the way? It was a guide of what to expect.

I now know to be careful when my internal barometer is falling. I know not to make any rash decisions. I know to carry on with care. And here's the really cool thing I've learned. The less I mess around with my internal barometer, in other words, the less involved I become in the content of my thinking, the quicker my state of mind rises. And once more I can connect back with my quiet mind.

7

TAKING THINGS PERSONALLY

BEA

How many times have you taken something someone said a bit too personally or interpreted it completely differently to how it was intended?

I'll be the first to admit that I have done so on numerous occasions. When I was unwell I did this a lot. I would always read into what someone was saying to try and figure out what they *really* meant.

When I was about 15, and I was in the thick of it with my anorexia, I remember going to visit some of my extended family and someone saying to me "Oh Bea, you look so well!" To anyone else this would have been music to their ears. I mean, who would not want to look well? Well, me. To me, this innocent comment meant that I had put on weight. It meant that I was failing.

During that time I very rarely took what people said to me on face value. To me there was always a deeper, hidden meaning that I had to try and figure out (because I'm such a great mind reader!) Unsurprisingly, this resulted in people feeling they had to choose their words extra carefully. Everyone was walking on eggshells, which turned out to be exhausting for everyone.

If anyone made any comment about what or how I was eating I would immediately go into self-destruct mode. I could be (relatively) happily eating something and one word anyone said about what I was doing would immediately make me want to stop. It would build up a feeling of resentment too. I was reading into and adding so much meaning to what people were saying, even if what they were saying was clearly well-intended. To me, there was always a hidden meaning.

Have you ever received a compliment and interpreted it to mean something negative? Or you start to dig into what you think they really meant by what they said? My guess is probably yes. But does it make you feel any happier or better about yourself? If so, feel free to skip to the next chapter. But from my experience, it can get pretty exhausting and it leaves you not feeling so great about yourself or the other person.

The good news is that, contrary to what most of us think, the words that come out of someone's mouth can't make you feel a certain way - it's us as individuals who add meaning to them. I imagine you are now probably thinking of lots of examples of where this isn't true, but bear with me.

When someone says something, they may well have their own hidden meaning behind their words. The family member who said "Oh Bea, you look so well!" could have really been thinking "Blimey she's put on a lot of weight. I knew she wouldn't be any good at this anorexia thing". It's highly unlikely, but it's possible. Yet despite her not actually saying that, I still reacted as if she did. So it wasn't the words themselves that I was reacting to, it was the story I made up whilst trying to read between the lines that made me feel the way I did.

And the fact of the matter is, as humans, we are incapable of reading other people's minds. We might like to think we can, and I often slip back into believing this, but we can't. So this means that we have a choice to make. We can either buy into the unhelpful stories we create, or we can realise what is really going on and then respond proportionately to what someone has actually said.

This may sound overly simplistic, but it's true. We may not always realise we have this choice, particularly as we will often react to something instantaneously, but just remembering that the option is there could save you a whole lot of stress and upset.

8

YOU ARE NOT YOUR STORY

REBECCA

I remember back to one early evening when Bea was ill. I was preparing dinner for the family. I was standing at the hob stirring something and deep in my own thought-filled world. I suddenly became aware of Dan, my youngest son, standing next to me, he was about 10 years old at the time. He had been calling my name for some time and I had been completely oblivious to him. I was so caught up in my own trance-like thinking about Bea and our situation that I didn't notice that he had been trying to attract my attention to ask me something. He had to shout in the end, pulling on my sleeve to get me to 'wake up'. I remember this so clearly, we both sat down on the kitchen floor and I gave him my full attention. Later that evening I cried as I wondered how much else I was missing.

Without even realising it, I was caught up in my own personal story, deep in thought about who knows what, but compelling enough for it to take me out of the present moment. Instead of listening to the story of Bea's illness and the impact it was having on our family, I could have been enjoying the moment with the family in the kitchen as I prepared dinner, listening to music, or helping out with homework. Instead I was imagining what the experience around the table later was going to be like. Would Bea eat? Would the atmosphere be tense? In reality I had no idea and worrying about it in advance was pointless. It's important to add in here that all of this was done innocently. There is no value in judging ourselves, or beating ourselves up. You and I are always doing the best we can in any one moment. And please don't think that I never get caught up in my thinking any more! I do! I've just come out of an episode of over-thinking that has resulted in a sleepless night!

Seeing that I/we are more than our stories would have been so much more helpful to have known back then. If I had felt that I didn't always have to appear strong or brave it might have helped us all a lot more than me believing I had to be a certain way in order to be 'the best' mother.

I had been plagued with feelings of low self-esteem much of my life. I didn't feel good enough in so many areas. I was stuck in looking to others, comparing myself with them and coming up short every single time (in my eyes). I wasn't clever enough, capable enough, organised enough, financially successful enough etc. You've probably got your own list.

Here's the blunt truth that I now see — *it's all made up*. All of it. Every single thought and belief we've had or still have about ourselves is made up. You aren't necessarily who you think you are, you absolutely aren't the negative story you've been telling yourself. Please stop and read this paragraph again whether you are someone with an eating disorder or someone caring for someone you dearly love. All the stories we have about ourselves are made up and we've innocently believed them to be true.

These stories, often elaborately created, make up the life we're currently living. The stories we often tell ourselves about not being good enough, not worthy of love, or food, or belonging, or friendships are the stories our insecure selves keep telling us as a way to keep us small, and hidden away. The thing is, we're here to shine our light, to share our gift with those around us. The playing small stuff comes from a place of fear.

You are not your personality, your story, your beliefs, your thinking, your history, the car you drive, your upbringing, the part of town you live in, your body, your exam results, your relationships, your career, your habits, or your feelings. You are so much more than that.

You might not be able to see this right now, but we, Bea and I, see you in your struggle. We know what it's like and although our experience is different to yours, we know what that fear and insecurity feels like. And it really doesn't have to be that way. There is healing, there is a way forward, there is recovery, full and complete.

We have all innocently created a world for ourselves where we believe the stories we hear in our head. We take the thoughts seriously. Insecurity, self-loathing, shame, worth-lessness... they are words, they aren't who we are. They are simply stories. Some thoughts and stories can have a positive impact, the ones where we see ourselves as confident, peaceful, at ease, worthy of love. It's up to you which you want to focus on. I'm more inclined to take notice of the ones that feel light rather than heavy. You can too.

The thoughts we have at night we call dreams. However real they are when we wake, we know it was a dream and we know not to take it seriously. Yet, the thoughts we have during the day, however outrageous or mesmerising they are, we accept them as reality and take them seriously. We then live with what we've created and call it 'my life'. It is an illusion.

You are worthy. You are loved. Even if you don't believe it, even if you can't imagine it, even if you're adamant that you're not. Let there be some tiny place within you that is prepared to question what you've believed in the past and right up until this moment.

Sometimes we're scared to even consider that we have more potential than we currently imagine for ourselves. We get scared that we have dreams and hopes and longings. Allow yourself to believe that you belong in the world, doing great things, fully engaged in being who you are, showing up in this one life you've been given.

As I mentioned earlier, I used to think that the weather affected my mood. That was one of my stories. I thought that the rain made me feel down and miserable and hopeless. I thought that the sun made me happy. I believed that for a long time until I saw that it wasn't true. This morning as I sit writing, it's pouring with rain, I've got the overhead lights on because it's so dark and it's the middle of the morning. And you know what? I'm happy, I'm laughing to myself because I'm feeling so at peace, productive, inspired AND it's pouring down with rain. Weird when I've made the assumption that the rain makes me miserable. I've also spent days when it's gloriously sunny and hot feeling very negative thoughts about myself and the world. It's never the weather.

Bea and I believe that everyone has innate wellbeing and the capacity to see it. Recovery doesn't have to be a struggle when we see that we innocently created the struggle with unhelpful thinking that we took seriously and acted upon. Every one of us is simply one thought away from having a completely new and different experience of life. Even you. Especially you right now in your struggle.

9

IF IT WEREN'T FOR THOUGHT BELIEVED

REBECCA

I feel very fortunate to live on the coast and to be able to watch day break and the sun rise out of the sea from my bedroom window. Some days it's raining. This is South Wales after all. Here's what came to mind as I was watching the sunrise on the sea front the other morning, cup of tea in hand.

I've always been curious to watch the sun rise because it's not actually happening the way we see it. In reality we are the ones moving towards the sun. Even though we know that, it still looks to me as if I'm watching the sun rise out of the sea.

We are also moving around the sun at 30 kilometres a second, and yet I don't feel dizzy or travel sick and I doubt you do either.

We're not seeing it (the sunrise) as it actually is but as *we* see it. And the same is true in life.

What we see as reality simply isn't always the case. It's a figment of our thinking that's been brought to life in our consciousness. I might see a piece of chocolate as something delicious and Bea looking at the same piece of chocolate might see it completely differently. It's extraordinary isn't it! And imagine too that every single person in the world is experiencing their own reality at the same time. Our entire experience of being alive comes to us via our thinking, brought to life in consciousness...and it's all made up!

If we can make the sunrise look real then imagine what we're doing day-to-day in the ordinariness of our lives.

That morning, I was curious about what else I'm seeing in life that isn't actually real and what I was thinking that wasn't actually true. I'm considering all the self-created suffering, all the stories that have accompanied me on my journey through life so far.

When Bea was ill, I now see that I was creating a lot of my own suffering, getting caught in thinking about what others might be thinking about Bea, about me and about us as a family. When I was scared, I looked for people and circumstances to blame, anything to take away the suffering. I was looking to the outside world to solve an 'inside' problem. What if I didn't believe that thinking and challenged those stories? How different would my experience have been at the time?

And what about Bea's suffering and the reason that any of us suffer? When we see that it's innocently caused by the stories that we've made up, then we can be free from them. I know now that these stories can seem utterly real and so ingrained that they don't even seem like thoughts anymore. And yet they are. Beliefs are simply thoughts that have taken hold and rooted themselves in our mind. However, this doesn't make them true. It's not until you get a glimpse of this yourself that they can loosen their grip. I can tell you this but it's not until you see it for yourself that you can be truly freed from them. Keep looking in this direction.

So what if you were to say to yourself, "If it weren't for believed thought, I would..." What would you see differently? What are you believing about yourself that you'd swear is fact and yet are prepared to get curious about?

If I'd done this exercise 10 years ago when Bea was ill I'd have focused more on what was wonderful in our lives. I'd have focused less on my perceived failings as a mother and more on the things that were going well in our lives. As it was, I believed all the negative things — my failing marriage, the difficult and painful relationship I seemed to have with Bea and how I felt out of control in my life.

What looks like fact to you right now? What could be different in your life now if you let go of the self-created suffering? The wonderful author, Byron Katie, urges you to "notice what unquestioned assumptions you are thinking." What if you did?

Why not pause a moment in reading this book and grab yourself a notebook or sit with someone you love and ask these questions? Bea and I do this now and again. We love calling each other out on our thinking! We love exploring this with each other because what we uncover moves us away from suffering and into a much more loving place. We've learned to have much more compassion and love for ourselves when we're prepared to challenge and question all the things we've believed. Life really doesn't have to be such hard work.

10

WHAT IS THOUGHT ANYWAY?

REBECCA

I have come to understand more and more profoundly over the past few years that the less I have on my mind the more peace, connection and love I feel within me and have in my life. The noise I used to experience in my head during the time of Bea's illness was like being in the middle of a busy marketplace, hundreds of voices yelling and shouting and screaming, all vying for my attention.

- Believe me, what I've got to say is important!
- No, I'm more important!
- You've got to listen to what I'm saying!
- Don't believe the other stuff!
- Me! Me! Me! Listen to me!

I got more and more involved in the content of my thinking. I was focusing on the minutiae of our daily lives rather than seeing the broader picture. I'd be focusing on what Bea might like to eat whilst at the supermarket, at the same time knowing that a fight was likely to ensue because I was going off script from the eating plan. I'd be worrying in advance about the possible conversation or conflict whilst walking down the aisles, hating it all. I'd be going through past conversations and shouting matches we'd had whilst out walking the dog, tears pouring down my face. All my relationships suffered because I was so caught up in my head that I was switched off from much of what was happening outside the family. And I felt judged for this.

I felt the louder this internal dialogue was speaking to me the more notice I needed to take of it. I would get to my bed at night utterly exhausted. I felt completely drained and my body was as stiff as a board. I was feeling every bit of my thinking and it was horrible.

What I didn't realise then was that thoughts come and go, constantly in flow. Let me explain. How many times have you headed upstairs on a mission to get something and have then promptly forgotten your reason for being upstairs? Then something else grabs our attention, you head back downstairs only to remember why you were up there in the first place. Sound familiar? That's the transient nature of thought in action. Always in motion.

Thought itself is also neutral. What I mean by this is that we are the ones who interpret our thinking. We make it either a negative, positive or neutral thought. Thought itself is a powerful, constant, creative force. It's always there and we have no control over it. Thoughts come and go all day long; we have no control over which ones come into our minds.

I was thinking more and more to try to find the solution to Bea's anorexia and her suffering. Surely as Bea's mother I should be able to make her better. Perhaps I wasn't working hard enough to find the solution. We all do that, don't we? We push harder, think more, exhaust ourselves. How many times have you driven somewhere and arrived with no real memory of driving? Have you sat in a meeting or with friends and someone's called your name and brought you 'back into the room'? Those are all examples of us being caught up in our thinking.

And then there are completely different moments, times when we fall out of our thinking. In my despair I'd sometimes find that I dropped out of all the noise. I'd switch off, I'd surrender. I don't mean I gave up but it felt deeper and more meaningful to sometimes no longer think about it. There were times I was absolutely done with thinking. You know, I'm sure there have been times in your life when you've just thrown your hands up in the air and just said, "I've no idea what to do next". It might be in a work context, or whilst studying or even within a relationship. The over-thinking seems to suddenly stop. And it's in this space of true surrender that answers appear. The answers appear somewhere other than where we've been looking. They appear from a place of wisdom, from the unknown, from somewhere in our unconscious mind. We call it insight.

Looking back this was true for me in how I parented Bea, the times I said to myself, I just don't know, I don't have the answer. This is when I would have these insights, this is when an idea to do something I'd never tried before came to me out of the blue.

The metaphor that stuck with me was seeing thought as the constant stream of headlines or breaking news that run along the bottom of the television screen on the 24-hour news channels. That's thought. It's always there. Most of the time we aren't focusing on it, we're watching and listening to the person on the screen. So in life, until something, often habitual thinking, grabs us and we find ourselves sucked into the drama of what is at that time unhelpful thinking. It's important to add in here that not all thinking is unhelpful! You'll know when thinking is helpful - it feels light and easy, you feel good about the thoughts coming through your head. I'm sure we've all suffered at some point from over-thinking. This feels totally different - heavy and unhelpful, claustrophobic in a way.

This isn't really about changing our thinking; rather it's about understanding the nature of thought. The answer isn't out there, and you don't need to buy any more self-help books! In fact, the answer isn't even in this book. The answer is within you. Recovery comes from within you.

When we see or even get a glimpse of the fact that thought is creating our reality and that we have a choice whether to believe and act on our compelling thoughts, it will no longer make sense for us to act on the thinking. You'll simply see it as thought and nothing more than that. And you will dip in and out. When we are in a negative state of mind we're much more likely to believe our thinking than when we're in a brighter and more positive state of mind.

If you've ever stood at a major railway station you know that some trains pass through without stopping. We're advised over the loudspeaker to stand back from the platform edge. Some trains slow down and we allow them to pass through because they're not heading where we want to go. Others we board. Sometimes we get on without even being sure whether it's the right train (surely it's not just me that's done that!) We can't control which trains pull into the station but we can decide which trains we board. It's the same with our thinking.

SECTION 2: FEELINGS AND EMOTIONS

"If the only thing people learned was not to be afraid of their experience, that alone would change the world."
~ Sydney Banks

Sadly, showing emotion is often seen as a weakness in our society. Showing emotion leaves us somehow vulnerable and this is considered weak. In British culture 'the stiff upper lip' has for far too many generations been the prescribed way to manage feelings. Young boys are told to "man up". Men are seen as soft if they cry. People are also often very uncomfortable when others show their emotions. We're almost embarrassed by people showing emotion in public. Children are hurried out of their feelings. "Don't cry", we tell them. "Don't get so angry. Be quiet. Stop making such a fuss." We've grown up learning this, and many of us innocently raise our children in this same environment.

We've learned to fear our emotions. We get scared to feel. Strong, powerful, stoic, unflappable, self-controlled — these attributes are seen as much more desirable than ones that are more expressive. And yes, there is a time and place for everything. However, everyone has emotions, no one is devoid of feelings. Emotions that are buried and go unacknowledged do eventually find an outlet. You just need to keep your thumb tightly over the end of a hosepipe to feel the buildup of pressure. The water will find a route out. The same is true for our emotions.

When we fear our feelings and emotions, we create any number of ways of hiding from them, of pushing them away. We find ways to numb our emotions. We become easily addicted to alcohol, to running, to self-harm, to bingeing or restricting in the hope that the feeling goes away.

We have learned so much about feelings and emotions these past couple of years, and no longer fear them. We're now able to feel them, all of them, and know that they pass. At times it might well feel like you're standing in the middle of a crazy storm, yet we all know that storms pass and the sun will eventually come back out again. In fact, in expressing our feelings and emotions rather than being controlled by them, we have discovered such freedom in our lives and from our suffering.

Whilst you read this section consider these three things:

- Feelings can't hurt us
- It is our thoughts that create our feelings
- It's okay to feel your emotions

11

WE'RE ALL LOOKING FOR A WAY TO FEEL BETTER

REBECCA

W hen Bea was diagnosed with anorexia, I felt so much pain. I felt helpless, and I had no idea why she would 'choose' to cause herself so much suffering. What kind of pain was she in that restricting her food intake seemed like the right decision to be making? I had no idea.

I too had suffered years of pain in the form of depression. Initially as an adolescent and then postnatally, which lasted on and off for about 10 years. I didn't know back then how the mind really worked and I blamed my feelings either on outside circumstances or my genetic makeup. My grand-mother and aunt had suffered from depression most of their lives, so perhaps I was the one in the next generation to be afflicted.

I really thought that I was somehow broken. I searched for a cure. I looked to the outside world — it's what we all do isn't it? I clearly thought I didn't have the answer at the time. I relied on medication for some time. It worked in that it took away the symptoms of depression, but it also numbed all my feelings and emotions. Medication did at least enable me to function on a daily basis — I had three children to take care of, a husband, and a home to look after. Therapy also helped, as it shone a light where before there had been only darkness, although I got to a point where I no longer felt it useful to keep going over old stories, adding more thinking to an already over-thinking mind. Where was that good feeling I longed for? There were moments where I caught a glimpse, but they were infrequent and my focus was on how dreadful I felt.

I went round in circles trying to solve my pain, wondering, worrying, stressing, trying to find the cause, the reasons. I wanted the pain I felt to go away. And when Bea was ill, I wanted to take away her pain too. It broke my heart that she should be suffering like this. I'd have done anything to ease her burden. That's not the way it works though. I was emotional and at times felt overwhelmed by the force of these feelings and tried to stop them from taking over.

What I didn't appreciate or know then was that it's not possible to fix a feeling; we can only wait for it to pass. Our feelings themselves can't hurt us. Think about that for a moment. It's not possible. They have no form or substance, yet we live our lives as if they hold power over us. Logically, sadness, anger, frustration, or jealousy as emotions are neutral. What we do with these emotions — the meaning we give them — is what causes our suffering. When I saw this for the first time and deeply understood it, I felt a huge relief. It was okay to feel the feelings, all of them, despair, fear, loneliness, sadness, regret, all of them. Yes, they could feel deeply painful but they couldn't hurt me or damage me in any way.

We're all happy to feel our positive, upbeat feelings most of the time aren't we? Although there are some I know who are anxious about being too happy because it's probably a sign that things will go wrong... how crazy are we really?!

I remember years back after heartbreak, I was terrified of crying, of letting out the emotion. My fear was that if I started crying, I wouldn't be able to stop. I really believed that it would break me somehow. I thought it would undo me and I'd fall apart. But I did cry, a lot. I didn't fall apart and I'm here to tell the tale. The fear of expressing the emotion is greater than the emotion itself. We tell ourselves that it's wrong to feel anger or frustration or resentment so we keep it inside, festering. We tell ourselves that pride is only a short hop to arrogance so we keep playing small. There are thoughts in our head that tell us that we'll never be as good, as clever, as accomplished, as successful, as whoever we've decided we need to be in competition with. So we punish ourselves.

Instead of expressing ourselves, having meaningful conversations, sharing our worries, our thoughts, we learn to keep our feelings inside. It's safer that way, we believe. We learn to be scared of our feelings and our emotions. There were times and with certain people when I'd wear a mask to hide my feelings. I didn't want others to see the pain we were going through. At times this became unbearable and I would run to my bedroom and sob, silently, until the pain inside eased. I'd wash my face and head back downstairs once more to face the music. Yes, it was good I let it out but it might have been better to do that in front of the family. Why did I feel I had to show this strong, invincible mask to the children when inside I was crumbling? I felt alone.

We're often looking to feel something different from what-ever we're feeling in the present moment. We want the present to be different. We say, "things will be better when..." We hate to feel discomfort and ill at ease. We'll do anything to *not* feel those emotions. The problem is that the more we focus on the feelings we don't want to feel, the deeper we fall into those feelings. It's just the way it seems to work.

We fight it. We numb it. We ignore it. It would be so much better if we acknowledged the pain, the feeling, surrendered to it, allowed it to pass through us, and expressed it in the moment.

Feelings are the embodiment of thoughts; it's our body's reaction to a thought. It's transient. Feelings aren't perma-nent once we let go of the need to fix them. And we must let go of that need, because there really is no way we can fix a feeling.

We sometimes look to bury or manage the feeling by taking medication or restricting or bingeing or self harming or drinking or excessively exercising or becoming addicted to sex or whatever 'thing' we look to as the 'cure' for our feel-ings. I longed to open the fridge for that first sip of wine in the evening, thinking that this would take away the pain. It did for a moment, but then I'd end up feeling worse, more in pain, more frightened. Wine wasn't the answer. Allowing myself to feel all the emotions freely would have been the answer; I didn't realise just how important that would have been to know then.

Thoughts trigger our feelings. Although neither thoughts nor feelings define who we are, they do create our experi-ence of life. When we become more aware that our thoughts don't need to be acted on, we are free to ignore the most unhelpful thinking we have. Let me give you an example. There were days when Bea was ill when I felt so alone, because no one around me understood what I was going through. My family didn't, Bea's father didn't, friends didn't. I did a lot of thinking about my loneliness, my isolation, my inability to cope and I had thoughts of running away and leaving them all to it, to sort out this mess... I could have taken these thoughts seriously, but I didn't.

The alcoholic becomes free when she realises that she doesn't have to listen to the mesmerising and insistent voice telling her that a drink will make her feel better or ease her pain.

The boy or girl is free to nourish their body once again when they no longer take seriously the voice that tells them that they'll only be loved when they are xx kilos or a size whatever.

12

COURAGE AND VULNERABILITY

BEA

W hen I was unwell I put up an emotional wall between myself and others. It was my defence mechanism. In my mind, if I expressed my emotions it meant that I was weak. It meant that people would think that I wasn't cut out for having an eating disorder. So I put up a wall to hide my vulnerability.

No one ever told me that showing my emotions meant that I was weak. In fact, no one ever told me that showing my emotions was anything other than a good thing. When I was growing up, Mum always encouraged me and my brothers to talk about our feelings. If we had a crap day or we were feeling low, we would talk about it. Looking back, I realise this isn't something that every family does and I feel lucky that we had the space to do so, free from judgment.

Like many people who don't quite fit the mould, I was bullied for a number of years when I was at school. I was excluded from my friendship group and nasty rumours were spread about me. School became a place that I dreaded. But I was fortunate in that I felt that I was able to talk about it and how it made me feel.

However, as time went on and I was diagnosed with anorexia, I became more closed off and stopped wanting to talk so much. My exterior started to harden so I wouldn't give away what was going on inside my head. This turned out to be pretty exhausting. I was using all my energy to keep my emotions under control, to not show my vulnerability.

Inevitably, as the pressure built up, cracks started to appear. It was like a dam that was ready to burst, and eventually it would get to the point where it did. When I felt that I couldn't hold it in any longer I would crumble, and all of the emotions I had been holding back would come rushing out. Giving into it felt like such a relief. For those moments, I was completely vulnerable, showing to the world that I desperately needed help. Mum said it was in these moments that she could see the 'real me' again.

But no sooner had the debris settled than I started to rebuild my fort. This process of collapsing and rebuilding was continuous, but Mum was always there to catch me. She was there to hold me when I was too exhausted to do anything but cry.

When I started to see a counsellor, an amazing woman named Elizabeth, I began to re-learn how to express my emotions. I learned to express them bit by bit instead of letting them build up and up until I hit saturation point.

What I lost sight of at the time was that no one was really going to judge me or think any less of me if I showed my emotions. I had made that up. It was just another one of my illusions. I also didn't realise that it was the stubbornness of my own thinking that was keeping me in that place. I was so caught up in my head, worrying about showing any kind of weakness, that I had forgotten that it was okay to show vulnerability. It takes courage to do that, a kind of courage that shouldn't be underestimated.

Brené Brown talks about this in her book "Daring Greatly: how the courage to be vulnerable transforms the way we live, love, parent, and lead". "Courage starts with showing up and letting ourselves be seen," she writes. This means presenting our "authentic, imperfect selves to the world" and in doing so, showing vulnerability. Only by doing this can we truly experience love and connection.

Now and again I catch myself allowing my stubbornness to get in the way of letting go of a particular thought or feeling. The other day, my boyfriend informed me that he had shrunk my favourite jumper in the wash. I know he didn't do it on purpose, but I was fuming and remained that way for several days because I wanted him to see how much it had annoyed me. Writing about it now makes me laugh because the only person I was really punishing was myself. I was digging my heels in, saying that I was going to be grumpy for the rest of the week, while he is quite happily elsewhere doing his own thing. Maybe I wasn't being so cunning after all.

Admitting this isn't the most comfortable of things to do. It takes courage to call out your own thinking. I think if I knew all those years ago that everything I was feeling was a direct result of my thinking, I maybe would have tried to challenge some of the thoughts that were swirling through my mind. I would have known that I didn't have to be afraid of my emotions.

When I felt like I needed help or just someone to talk to, I had to ignore the voice in my head telling me that I shouldn't. I had to pluck up the courage to voluntarily show my vulnerability, at the risk of looking weak or being judged. I would have a mental back and forth, weighing up whether it was worth the risk, using more thinking to battle my thinking.

I feel that courage was a vital part of my experience of dealing with anorexia. What may seem like a simple task to some would take a huge amount of strength from me to do. I remember clearly on my 16th birthday my Mum made a mountain of chocolate brownies as my birthday cake. I loved chocolate brownies (and still do), especially the ones Mum makes. They were perfectly gooey and not too sweet, but I hadn't eaten them for a long time, years in fact. I didn't allow myself to. They were pretty high up my blacklist so were a definite no-go. But something happened on my birthday that made me want to try them again. I had my mental battle, but after a while I broke off a corner and ate it. The inevitable feelings of guilt ensued but I had plucked up the courage to try it and to nudge at the walls of my comfort zone. These were baby steps — and to this day I still remember the feeling of pride I got from doing it.

What I know now is that embracing vulnerability, and finding the courage to do so, is essential to living a happy, fulfilled life, no matter who you are or whether you suffer from an eating disorder or struggle with something else. Vulnerability is a fundamental part of being human and, as Brené Brown says, "it fuels our daily lives".

13

LOVE AND FEAR

REBECCA

"Whatever the question, love is the answer."
~ Dr. Wayne Dyer

Marianne Williamson is one of my favourite spiritual writers. Her piece which begins, "Our deepest fear is not that we are inadequate, our deepest fear is that we are powerful beyond measure..." was pinned up in the kitchen whilst Bea and her brothers were growing up. If you don't know it, I'd encourage you to look it up. There's so much within her words that inspires me and perhaps they'll resonate with you too.

Another of her quotes is this one, which feels particularly relevant to what we're sharing with you: "Love is what we are born with. Fear is what we learn." It's something I believe wholeheartedly. We're not born in a state of fear. Fear is a learned feeling and, sadly, one that too many people spend their life in, making their lives miserable and full of effort.

How many of us make decisions from this place of fear

and low state of mind? We leave a job, we leave a relationship, we end a friendship. I lived in fear a lot of the time when Bea was ill. I was scared. I'd read the statistics, I'd done my research. I knew that this wasn't going to be easy. I could let my mind run away with me during those times when I was terrified that my daughter might end up in hospital on a drip. Thinking about it today still brings me to tears. My fear was that Bea was so good at everything in life that she'd also be 'good' at anorexia. That was my deepest fear.

The problem is that when we're in this fearful thinking place our naturally buoyant minds are closed down. We isolate ourselves from those around us who love us. We become scared of life; it looks too painful to face, in case we find other things that hurt us. Our focus becomes narrowed, we stop noticing other things in life that are happening around us. In a way it felt like my mind was on standby, simply doing what was immediately in front of me, fighting fires every day. My mind was filled with noise. I felt incredibly insecure at times, unable to handle my own fearful emotions let alone be there to support Bea and the family around me.

On the surface it seemed like my fear was coming from the statistics, or Bea's refusal to eat, or the conversation with the psychiatrist, the therapist or the nutritionist. It really did look that way. And yet that's not possible. My experience was coming from *my* fearful thinking about the situation or the circumstances. Bea's experience of all the above will have been totally different. My emotions, moods and, feelings are only ever coming from my personal thoughts. Likewise with Bea. Likewise with you. We all have separate realities, all 7.6 billion human beings on this planet, all thinking, all feeling, all having different experiences of being alive.

When we make decisions from this fear-filled place, the decisions often won't be wise, because they are a reaction to something 'out there'. We're starting off on the back foot, already caught up in negative thoughts and feelings. It's already starting off as a clouded decision, and it's never going to feel good.

We fear the unknown, don't we? We don't like uncertainty. We're scared of change. We want proof that it's all going to work out okay. We fantasise about an unknown future and make it real in our thinking. And yet, none of this is true. We have absolutely no idea how things will actually play out, and yet we continue to torture ourselves with thinking and imagining, dramatising and fearing.

This might seem a giant leap, but what a relief to know and to see that love is the flip-side. I know it's a cliché and I make no excuse for it, because love really is the answer.

I used to notice the difference in Bea, in her body language and how she spoke when we headed to our appointments. She hated it. She shut down and it often felt directed at me, because, well, I was the one driving us to the hospital. I now see that I could love her through all this, through the words, the heavy silences, and see it simply as her fear being acted out. She was scared. I was scared. We expressed our fears differently. When I loved unconditionally without expecting anything in return, I felt better and would often find that Bea reacted differently. When we are free of the expecta-tions we place on ourselves and others, we're all much more able to communicate from a better place.

When we are able to live from a place of love and under-standing so much more seems possible. There is hope; it's the most beautiful of words. There is always hope. I actually feel I have more room in my mind and my body when I see the difference between fear and love. I was at the beach a few months ago; it's a huge beach about five miles from one end to the other. When I looked one way I could see a dark, brooding sky with jet black clouds; it made me want to pull my jacket around me to protect myself from the impending storm. I turned and looked the other way and I saw nothing but blue sky. Seriously, it was extraordinary. It was a beau-tiful representation of what I'm talking about here. Fear vs. Love.

All I could do was love Bea, wholly, unconditionally, and unreservedly with all my heart. I loved her, whatever thinking she was believing. When I was in that space in my mind it felt much more hopeful. I had a quieter mind and felt much more creative in how I handled not only myself but the illness.

There is always a quieter mind when we are coming from a place of love. We are much more able to communicate effec-tively from this state of mind. We can still be fearful, but we don't feel so paralysed by it. The mind stills naturally. Love is the default setting for us. Newborn babies teach us this beautifully; they know all about love, they don't doubt love for a moment. When they get fearful, for example, when the dog barks or someone rings the doorbell, they get scared and then it passes and they're back in their natural state of bliss and love. We, on the other hand, hang out in the fearful place. We've told ourselves that that is our default. It's not. We know this space of love, every one of us, what-ever thinking you've got about that right now!

I know it sounds too good to be true but it really is the place to start. I also knew that I had to begin with myself, loving myself wholeheartedly, even the bits I didn't like about myself. I had to love the fact that I was struggling too, no judgments, embracing my frailties as a mother, even embracing and loving myself through the fact that some days I just wanted to run away. Loving all the stuff I felt guilty about, all my perceived shortcomings. All of it. You see, my thinking was keeping me in a place of fear. If I could see my thinking as not who I was, then I could let it go. I had to learn to see it as transient and get back to a place of love — for myself and for my daughter. Love is always, always the answer.

14

TRUST AND ANGER

BEA

Trust is a funny thing when it comes to eating disorders. When I had anorexia, I didn't trust anyone and no one trusted me. I didn't trust Mum to weigh out my food correctly; I didn't trust her to not use extra butter and oil in her cooking to add in more calories. The very nature of having an eating disorder meant that no one could trust me either. Given how hard I tried to deceive, I know there was an underlying feeling of mistrust towards me from my family and the doctors. It didn't help when I got caught hiding food — any gains we had made in terms of building trust would evaporate. We'd be back to square one. I don't blame them for not trusting me. If I was in their position I wouldn't have trusted me either. But the inability for either 'side' to trust the other meant we were constantly walking on eggshells. One was always suspicious of the other.

Deep down, I think I knew Mum and the doctors had my best interests at heart. At times I could see their good intentions more clearly than at others. It was in these moments that my angry and resentful thoughts weren't quite so loud. I was angry because no one trusted me; I was angry because I had to be constantly monitored; sometimes I was angry at the fact that I was angry all the time; sometimes I didn't even know why I was angry.

Do you ever find yourself in a bad mood with someone and you can't remember why, but you feel that you have to continue being in a mood with them because if you break character you fear you'd look a bit silly? I felt like this a lot. I so often felt that I had to continue expressing a particular emotion like anger, because otherwise it would have exposed the cracks in my persona. If I wasn't sleeping or crying I was probably being angry at someone or something. It was like anger had become my default setting.

One of the things that made me most angry was being policed all the time. In my eyes, Mum had become my prison guard — very little got past her. I know she hated having to play this role but she and I both knew that I couldn't be trusted to stick to the rules laid out by the hospital. She would weigh out my cereal in the morning and monitor me while I ate it. She would sit with me while I ate my snack. She would check up on me during the day to make sure I wasn't exercising. And it only made it worse when others were recruited to police me on her behalf. I remember staying at my aunt and uncle's house in South Wales and my aunt had to administer my afternoon snack while Mum wasn't there. I knew she had to do it but I hated that in doing so she became 'one of them'.

I remember feeling very protective of my eating disorder. It was something I had worked hard on, so whenever someone tried to take it away from me (i.e. by making me eat), anger and resentment would bubble up. The image of Gollum protecting the ring in The Lord of the Rings springs to mind! Mum often described me like this when I was ill. One moment I could be gentle and friendly like Sméagol and then next I could be hissing through my teeth like Gollum.

I always denied having two sides to my personality. I insisted that anorexia wasn't another side to me — I couldn't see the separation. I believed that it was me. Looking back I now see that neither was true. Anorexia wasn't who I was. My anger, my Gollum moments, were merely the result of a torrent of angry thoughts that were swirling through my mind. I didn't know that at the time. I didn't know where my often inexplicable rush of anger came from. I would try pinning it on something or someone. It was the weighing scales; it was the doctor; it was something Mum said that put me in a bad mood. But I know now that this is not how it works.

I know now - as we've said a few times already in this book - that our thoughts create our feelings. End of. We can't experience a feeling without having a thought. This means that nothing 'out there' can directly make us feel anything. Something Mum says can trigger some thinking that will result in me feeling something, but her words alone don't have the power to make me feel angry. She could say the exact same thing to someone else and they could have a completely different reaction. That's because our thinking about what she said is different. If she said, "You need to eat this piece of toast" to me and my brothers, my reaction could be to fly into a rage about how unfair it is that she has to force me to eat, while my brothers could rub their hands together with glee before scoffing it down in one go.

The other day I saw this so clearly. I was on holiday and I

suddenly thought about having to go back to work. In that instant, I suddenly went from feeling totally chilled out to feeling anxious and sick. It was instantaneous. I had a thought and it made me feel sick. Nothing on the outside had changed. I was sitting in exactly the same place, doing exactly the same thing. All that had changed was that a new thought had come into my head. And as quickly as that thought had popped into my head, it left again and I carried on as I was before.

The difference between this experience and other times where I've experienced anxious thinking is that I didn't get involved with these thoughts — I didn't start to interrogate them or give them so much attention. I didn't obsess over feeling anxious. I didn't start picking apart why I was experiencing feelings of anxiety or why I was worried about going back to work. I just didn't follow my thinking down the usual rabbit hole that lands me in an unhelpful state of mind where I don't know what's up or down.

15

HOPE AND ANXIETY

REBECCA

"Seize any feeling of hope and trust it, for hope is the seed that will germinate a new life." ~ Joseph Bailey in The Serenity Principle

Hope is one of the most powerful words in the English language. Without hope what is there? Hopelessness and despair. We had originally decided to use despair as the opposite for hope in this chapter but when it came to writing I realised that I never actually felt despair when Bea was ill. Despair, to me, means that all hope has been extinguished and this was never the case. I now know that this never need be the case for any one of us. We all have the capacity for a new thought, a fresh insight that takes us from despair to hope in a moment.

The feeling I experienced was much more akin to anxiety. Anxiety is everywhere, it's at epidemic levels in our schools and workplaces. I see this very differently now because of my understanding of the source of anxiety. I'm no longer frightened by it. Let me explain.

At times anxiety used to control me. I've experienced panic attacks and such intense anxiety that I've literally had to leave a room running. I felt like I was being taken over by the intensity of the feeling; the fear associated with it was terrifying to me. I've sat in a fancy restaurant, not actually sure I could swallow because my anxiety was so great. I've been on the verge of standing up to give a presentation and the noise in my head was so loud I had to make my excuses and leave.

The anxiety I felt at times when Bea was ill was almost over-whelming. My body ached with the tension I held in it. I went to see a friend of mine, a sports massage therapist, and she was visibly taken aback at the stiffness in my body. As she massaged by tense muscles, I began to soften along with my muscles and we both cried as the anxiety and tension began to leave my body.

When Bea was ill there was so much noise in my head, fearful thinking, anxiety, all tied up in insecurity and uncer-tainty and not knowing what to do or how to behave. Add into that mix the others around me who were anxious too, and me feeling like I had to be the strong one. I felt pulled in every direction and was losing sight of who I was, that calm and collected woman who I knew was in there somewhere... except for when I felt I totally lost touch with her.

When I was feeling anxious it was like being in a dark tunnel and not knowing the way out. I'd go around in circles that took me deeper into the pain and suffering. I'd get glimpses of daylight, of hope. There would be moments of laughter, of lightheartedness and these would keep me going on dark days.

Anxiety felt like a physical burden I was carrying around

with me. I longed to put it down but was too frightened to do so. I felt that the weight was what I had to feel, the weight I believed was keeping me alert to signs that Bea was deteriorating; it was what kept me awake. My body was running on adrenaline a lot of the time, but our bodies are not designed for this. Cortisol, the stress hormone, is only meant to be released in extreme life and death times, like when we're being chased by a tiger! My body was on high alert all the time. My shoulders were tense, my breathing was shallow and my head hurt.

Here's what I've now learned about anxiety (hindsight is a wonderful thing). Anxiety is an uncomfortable feeling, which has been triggered by a thought. I realised much later on that I didn't need to fix a bad feeling. Seeing that anxiety is simply a series of thoughts would have freed me from needless suffering.

There is a natural ebb and flow of our feelings; some days I'd feel anxious and other days I'd feel hopeful. Thinking I needed to fix the anxious days was an innocent misunderstanding of where the anxiety was coming from. I was creating and hanging on to the anxiety, and in doing so I was making it mean something when really there was no meaning to it at all. Just like the tide comes in and out, the flow of my thinking and feelings is completely natural. Trying to fix them would be like trying to stop the outgoing or incoming tide.

It's the resistance to the feelings that causes us to suffer. Resistance feeds them. Resistance gives them power. We think they must mean something, that we must take more notice, greater care, be more on guard, keep alert. We get exhausted fighting and resisting. Yet when we truly realise where those feelings are coming from, we can see them for what they are. They are thoughts, and thoughts by their very nature are fluid, they come and go.

I was feeling anxious because I was having anxious thoughts. The feelings weren't coming from the situation, from the circumstances of Bea's eating disorder, they were coming from the thinking I had. The fact that Bea was ill triggered thoughts in me that caused me to feel something unsettling and painful. It was only ever coming from my thinking. I didn't know this at the time and would understandably get completely lost in anxiety.

One day Bea would make progress (in my eyes) and I'd feel hopeful; she'd be angry or confrontational the next and I'd feel anxious again. Although it looks like it was Bea causing those feelings in me, I know it was only my interpretation of what she was doing or saying. It was my thinking about the situation.

I would lurch between hope and anxiety as if I were a pendulum. We fall over, it's part of life, we do it often and yet we have the inbuilt capacity to get back up again — our resilience is built in. It really does come as part of the package of being human. We often forget this and it's only when we remember that we can settle back into neutral and the pendulum can find its equilibrium.

We don't have to suffer so much. We can feel pain — this is natural — but we don't need to be frightened by it when we know where it's coming from. We are deeply okay even when we're consumed by the anxiety.

Hope is like love, it's expansive, it's creative, it's open, it's freeing. Like love, hope is more likely to be felt when we are peaceful and have less on our mind. It's a place of serenity. I know now that I was a much more helpful mother and caregiver when I was in this place rather than when I was wound up, anxious and exhausted.

When I felt hopeful, everything felt easier. Bea and I would be able to enjoy each other's company doing all the things we liked to do together — creative projects, walking the dog, watching films.

We often describe ourselves as being an anxious person as if it's who we are. It's not true though. We aren't ever permanently anxious. My silver hair, blue eyes and being 5' 6" is as permanent as it gets right now, not my mood or how I'm feeling in a single moment. The truth is that there are always going to be moments during the day when we're not anxious. The same goes for addictions. During the time a client isn't thinking about alcohol he's not an alcoholic. During the times that you're not thinking about weight or food you are not anorexic. We all get caught up in our thinking and have thoughts and feelings, moods and emotions that take us towards our addiction or illness, but it is not who we are.

There is always hope. In each moment we have the possibility for a new thought which will move our feelings and emotions forward.

16

RESILIENCE AND INSECURITY

REBECCA

W hat if you could see something that you may not have seen before? What if you could see that resilience is your natural state of being? I promise you that the moment you realise this, life never looks the same again. Nothing 'out there' has the power to knock your innate wellbeing and resilience.

There's a quote I've seen many times which goes like this, "on particularly rough days I like to remind myself that my track record for getting through bad days is 100%, and that's pretty good." Isn't that true? Go ahead, copy it out and keep it taped to your cupboard or somewhere you'll see it every day. You've made it through every single day. If that isn't resilience then I don't know what is.

We really don't give ourselves the credit we're due when it comes to resilience. It's within us naturally, there's nothing we have to do apart from see it and appreciate it as part of us. It's who we are. When we look back on it now, both Bea and I were incredibly resilient (as are you right now). Bea came through the toughest experience of her life, we came through the toughest experience of our lives and even in the direst of moments, deep down, we were okay. We might not have seen it that way back then, just as you might well be questioning your own resilience right now too. Read that quote again in the previous paragraph. Remind yourself of it.

Google the word resilience and you'll come across more articles and advice than you could ever read. There are plenty of people who have advice for you on how to become more resilient. Innocently they're pointing you away from your own, pre-existing wellbeing and resilience. Your resilience is built into your operating system.

So where does insecurity fit in? Well, sitting here on the sofa talking it through with Bea, we felt that the reason many of us feel so insecure is because we've forgotten just how resilient we are. And so we go out looking for ways to feel less insecure. We numb, we hide, we become addicted, we turn to others believing that security lies with them. You'll know what you use as your security blanket. This makes so much sense when we don't realise that we're resilient by nature.

Insecure thinking is the cause of our struggles in relationships and in life. Here's what we've come to see and believe — that insecurity resides only in our thinking. We cannot actually feel insecure without having insecure thoughts. When we have insecure thinking we feel unloved, disconnected, and alienated. We feel all those other feelings that take us away from who we really are, which increases our sense of insecurity.

When we see that our feelings of insecurity are not coming from someone else's Instagram feed, what someone supposedly said about us, a comment from our boss, or grades in an exam, then we are much more able to connect with our own wisdom and resilience. When we see that our thinking alone is what we're experiencing (and that could look like insecurity right now) then life starts to look a lot more manageable.

17

IT'S OKAY TO FEEL OKAY

BEA

When I was ill I got used to feeling crap all the time. I got used to feeling angry, upset and worn out most days of the week. I would go through phases of not remembering what it was like not to feel that way. I'm not telling you this to try and win your sympathy, far from it. I'm telling you this because when I was ill I didn't know that it didn't have to be this way.

I thought that being happy, positive and energetic would show cracks in my illness. It might make people think that I was getting better and I didn't need the help and attention I so desperately craved. It might hint at the fact that deep down on a fundamental level I really was okay.

But it's okay to ignore those misleading thoughts and just go with the good feeling. It's okay to embrace the positive feelings when they come along and give yourself time off from feeling anxious or worried or angry.

I now know that it's okay to show vulnerability, and I also know that it's okay to show that you are okay and to not feel that you're stuck in an endless cycle of negative feelings and emotions.

Even if we feel a certain way the majority of the time, it doesn't mean this is the way we're meant to feel or that it's the default. We're not born that way. But actually, happiness isn't the default either. I think our minds are always trying to get back to neutral. We can feel some pretty extreme emotions — both positive and negative — but when we're not caught up in the thoughts that are creating those feelings, we will automatically fall back into our neutral state of 'okayness'.

Before I had anorexia, I thought that I had to try to be happy all of the time, and that if I wasn't then something must be wrong. But, just as I've said in this chapter that it's okay to break character and feel happy and positive, it's also okay to just be okay. It's also okay to not feel okay at all.

Previously I'd always tried to do something about the way I felt. I would try to make myself feel happy; I would even sometimes try to make myself feel upset or angry. But what I was missing was that actually, we can give ourselves permission to feel whatever it is that we're feeling in that moment. Eventually, we'll automatically get back to neutral, but the longer we spend trying to fix how we feel, the longer it'll take us to get there.

You may be feeling that you're being sold short here and that you want to feel more than just OK. The good news is that you can — you're only one thought away. But the reassuring thing is that it's okay to feeling exactly how you're feeling right now.

18

DON'T BE SO FRIGHTENED TO FEEL

REBECCA

This chapter was a late and (what I now see as) very important addition to the book. As Bea and I came to the end of the first draft of writing, we went back through it to clarify sections. We tweaked and deleted things that no longer made sense to keep in the book. Bea pointed out to me that in places I was very much writing from the perspective of a coach rather than as a mother and carer. I was writing from a detached place rather than being fully involved. I thought I was showing vulnerability but realised that as Bea wrote about in the chapter 'Courage and Vulnerability' I too was metaphorically wearing a mask in my writing. And that is of no help to you whatsoever.

I feel this is really important to share with you and reiterate what Bea has said in the previous chapter — don't be frightened to feel whatever it is you're feeling. Without realising it I was neglecting my own needs to share what it was like for me as a carer because I didn't want this book to be about me. I was seeing this book as Bea's recovery rather than mine or even ours.

The first draft didn't include many of my experiences as a carer because I didn't feel it should. This, in a way, is the very reason why carers suffer so much and why I've now woven my feelings, stories, and vulnerabilities into the book. You see, it is often the carers who don't feel they can talk about how it is for them because they think the focus should be solely on the one needing care.

I wasn't taking my self-care seriously enough. I now see with such clarity that the carer needs to be well and have a clear mind. This only comes when we're less caught up in our thinking. It comes when we're getting on with life and not focusing our entire waking moments on anorexia. It comes when we look after our own personal needs. When we have a clearer mind, something about how we act and behave seems to rub off on those around us. In a way it's almost more important that you, the carer, see what Bea and I are pointing to about our innate wellbeing and how we really experience life, because you are then able to share what you see with the person you're caring for. Bea said that when she was in the thick of anorexia she had so much noise in her head that she was unlikely to even pick up a book to read. Perhaps if I'd been more present in my emotions, looking after myself and had an understanding of how the mind works, then even unconsciously I'd have been a better role model for her and she would have been more likely to take note.

When Bea was ill I felt totally isolated. People rarely asked me how I was (and even writing that causes me to have some unhelpful internal dialogue about it not being about me anyway!). The focus is on the patient rather than the carer. Yet, the carer *needs* to be well both physically and mentally. I neglected my own needs. I bottled everything up. I didn't show vulnerability and now in my writing I'm learning to do so.

It was so hard at times, I do want you to know that. And I want you to know that it's okay for you to feel that too. Writing about it now I'm taken back to those times, and I have tears in my eyes. There were times I wasn't sure I had the strength to look after Bea. I was also struggling because Bea's anorexia wasn't the only thing going on in our lives at the time. Things never happen in isolation. My marriage was on the rocks — my relationship with Bea's dad was terrible and there was a lot of bitterness and resentment. My eldest son, Ollie, had left home for university and his first year was tough for him given everything that was going on at home. My youngest son, Dan, was struggling in school and one of the reasons I now believe to be the cause was that he was coming to terms with his sexuality at the time... and the supermarket shop still needed to be done and new school shoes bought.

I was exhausted and still I kept on being strong. You will have your own version of this. It's okay to admit that it's really hard. It's okay to admit that there are days that you don't feel you have any strength left.

I was also trying to manage the worries and concerns for the rest of the family. I was spinning plates that weren't actually mine to spin! But I kept on spinning them because I didn't know what else to do.

What would have been helpful for me to know 10 years ago was that it's not just okay to show our feelings, it's healthy to show them, whatever they may be. I didn't have to wear the mask all the time. Perhaps by me being more vulnerable Bea might have seen that she too could be vulnerable. Who knows what might have happened then along her road to recovery. I wonder how differently I might have handled everything that was happening around me if I'd understood what we're sharing with you now. I'm sure those really dark days wouldn't have felt so oppressive. I'm sure I'd have seen that it wasn't my marriage or Bea's refusal to eat that was causing my anxiety and suffering.

19

F.I.N.E - F*CKED UP, INSECURE, NEUROTIC, AND EMOTIONAL

REBECCA

A nd then there are all those times when we've said 'I'm FINE' when we are anything but fine. What is the point in telling people we're FINE when we're feeling absolutely f*cked up, insecure, neurotic, and emotional (the acronym in Aerosmith's song F.I.N.E)? The times when I was real and vulnerable enough to no longer play the 'strong' game, here's what I felt.

F*cked up — I was so caught up in my thinking most of the time. Anorexia and my darling daughter were the first things I thought about on waking and the last thing I thought about as I fell asleep utterly spent and exhausted. And that 3 a.m. thinking that is usually like living through some horror story at the best of times, well, that too. It was like some giant ball of wool that was in an unfathomable knot. The more I tried to loosen the knots the tighter it got. I just wanted to hurl the whole thing across the room and out of my life. I didn't want this to be happening to us. Why us? There were times that I just wanted to scream like some wild woman. The pain I felt was immense. As a mother I couldn't do anything, it seemed, to heal my daughter. I couldn't make this go away. We were living through a f*cking nightmare.

Insecure — I had so much insecure thinking. What I thought of myself hadn't been great even before we were in this chaos following years of protracted postnatal depression. Just as I was getting myself back together again (I was beginning my coaching training at the time) we were being punched in the stomach by anorexia. I felt like I was walking on a tightrope with no safety net. Was it the fact that Bea's dad and I were in a very unhappy place in our marriage? Was it that my encouragement of a bright child had felt pushy? Was it that I loved too much and she felt stifled? Was it something I'd said once in the heat of the moment? Was it my depression that had somehow seeped through me and into her? Was it the 'middle child' syndrome? Every day I'd latch on to one or many of these questions and beat myself with it. I felt such guilt and shame.

Neurotic — Anxiety was a daily state of being. My heart raced, I was short of breath all the while trying to hold it together for everyone else. I felt at my breaking point much of the time and yet somehow managed to continue, to get to the end of a day and wake the next day. Day by day by day we made it to the end of the day. Sleep, when it came, was my solace. I became neurotic about Bea watching my every move when it came to mealtimes. It felt like Big Brother watching over me all the time.

Emotional — This was such a difficult game we played. I felt I needed to give off an air of strength, nothing was going to scare me, I remember telling Bea this one day, when I was speaking directly to the anorexia. NOTHING WILL SCARE ME. And yet I was an emotional wreck inside. I'd take myself to my bedroom and sob into my pillow so that I couldn't be heard. I was terrified of showing emotion because I didn't want to come across as weak or unable to cope. I was like a pressure cooker whose valve is about to explode. And the thing is that when I did 'blow' I felt better. The world didn't come to an end. It was like pressing the reset button. I was able to cope. Life went on.

That was then and this is now with a very different understanding of how the mind works. Not a day goes past without the words of Sydney Banks resonating in my ears, *"If the only thing people learned was not to be afraid of their experience, that alone would change the world."* Well, it changed my world, that's for sure.

Our experience, our feelings can't hurt us and yet we live in a world where we go around as if they do. I was having f*cked up, insecure, neurotic, and emotional thinking that was leading to me feeling f*cked up, insecure, neurotic, and emotional. It wasn't saying anything about me as a person. And even if I'm feeling all those things I know now that it's not permanent. Thought is transient, and it certainly can't control or make me do something. I don't have to believe or act on my thinking and neither do you.

SECTION 3: IDENTITY

"As long as you make an identity for yourself out of pain, you cannot be free of it."
~ Eckhart Tolle

What do we mean when we talk of identity? I guess when asked, we'd answer by saying, "It's who I am." But who are you really? Are you your beliefs, your thoughts, the things you're good at, your personality, your experiences? Or are you something more than that?

What you think of yourself one day or one moment can flip to the opposite the next. One moment it's possible to believe yourself to be a great parent or friend, the next, after a disagreement with someone you love, you view yourself as a dreadful person. You may be articulate one moment and utterly unable to string a sentence together the next; kind, considerate, and generous one moment and bitter, resentful, and mean the next. So, who are you really?

Have you ever thought that what we think of ourselves is not what others think of us? Who they see is not who we see?

What they think is not what we think? We create versions of ourselves and others in our heads. In reality none of them are real. What I think of you is not the same as what you think of yourself. What you think of me is not what I think of myself. Can you see? It's all a case of mistaken identity. So, take a moment to wonder who you are really.

The more we dived in to exploring what identity meant for us, the more we came to see how we limit ourselves with erroneous labelling. We see how easily we box ourselves into an identity that closes us off from so much of life. We are so much more than the identity we've labelled ourselves with. We are innocently carrying on with our lives whilst believing things about ourselves that simply aren't true. And it's causing needless suffering.

Bea wasn't the anorexia. Yes, she had an eating disorder, there was absolutely no denying that, her BMI, her hair loss, her freezing hands and feet told us so.

We take on the negative attributes of our identity so readily. We don't often use positive words to describe ourselves. For many of us it feels strange to do so. We feel self-conscious at best and deeply uncomfortable at worst. We often find it hard to identify things we are really good at, or things we like, let alone love, about ourselves. To share words around what we appreciate about ourselves with others leaves us feeling vain, arrogant, or untruthful.

All of it is made up. Our identity, our thoughts, our beliefs. All of it. We really don't need to believe any of it.

Jack Pransky, Three Principles author says, *"All we are is love, peace, and wisdom and the power to create the illusion that we're not."* This is really beautiful; it's the truth we both see.

Imagine living life knowing this. Seeing yourself in this way might well be a huge struggle right now. What if you could simply hold that idea somewhere in your mind, simply saying 'what if' to yourself?

Whilst you read this section consider these three things:

- Notice how your current beliefs about yourself may be keeping you playing small
- What would change if you saw yourself as more than your current 'identity'?
- What if you didn't take the stories you're telling yourself about who you are so seriously?

20

WE AREN'T WHO WE THINK WE ARE

REBECCA

I was training to become a coach during the time that Bea had anorexia. It felt good to be surrounded and supported by others who didn't really know me. I was able to relax a bit, to not have to be known as someone in particular. They didn't know my history, my background, whose mother or daughter or sister I was. In a way I was identity-less. I could be whoever I wanted to be when I showed up to the course. I could be anyone.

One of the lessons I learned from this and for which I'm grateful was my ability to see more clearly that Bea was not her illness. I knew that she wasn't 'anorexia' and as such it didn't have to be a life sentence — and this comforted me. Of course there were days when I really struggled to see this. The days she and I fought over what was on her plate. Those days I found it hard to see beyond the illness.

When Bea was ill I created a playlist of songs that had a deeper meaning in their lyrics. I'm not even sure Bea knew I'd done this! "Shine" by Take That was on the playlist. Look up the lyrics when you have a minute. They represented everything I longed for her to see about herself and yet knew that she was so entrenched in her own identity thinking that at the time she wasn't able to hear them. I'd play it when I was in the car alone, tears streaming down my face as I tried to sing along.

Even then I still knew anorexia wasn't who she was. We can tell someone something that we know is true, but until they hear or see it for themselves all we can do is love them unconditionally. This love we demonstrate by being there for them unconditionally, trusting they'll see that they truly aren't the stories they've made up about themselves.

When we look at an Ordnance Survey map we see lines, some close together, some further apart. It's a two dimensional representation of the terrain. It's not the landscape. It's just the same for us. We aren't who we think we are. We are more than the words we use to describe ourselves. We don't realise how much we are limited by the stories we continually tell ourselves.

- I am more than being an eldest daughter to ageing parents
- I am more than being a divorced mother of three children
- I was more than the mother of a daughter with an eating disorder
- I am frankly more than anything I choose to write after 'I am'

And so are you. And so is Bea.

We've grown up with an identity, components of which we've collected during our life. We've listened to things we've overheard, we've listened to our parents, we took on board something our boss or teacher or friend said and absorbed it into our identity.

"I'm the sort of person who..." becomes our soundtrack. And it's interesting isn't it because it's usually the limiting beliefs that we take seriously, not the empowering ones. Imagine a world where the reverse was true for us all.

From a carer's perspective we can offer a very different and much more helpful type of support when we see beyond the labels that are given to or used by our loved one to identify themselves. Note also that the same applies to us. We are so much more than the labels we've attached to ourselves that relate to our loved one's illness or suffering. Perhaps if I'd not labelled myself as the strong, in control, resilient super-woman I might have not struggled so hard when I didn't live up to those words. I'd made all that up and I was suffering because of it.

I remember clearly one day someone asking me why I allowed Bea to speak to me the way she did. We'd just had a horrible argument about food and portion sizes and I was at the end of my tether again. The thing is, I just knew not to take the attack personally. I knew that it wasn't Bea talking, it was the eating disorder. They were two separate things. Knowing this on a fundamental level was my lifesaver. Bea was reacting to thinking she had and pushed it out onto me. We've all done it, haven't we. We've all said something we didn't really mean to someone we love. When we're hurting or in pain we say and do hurtful things. It's a human thing.

I felt so alone because no one seemed to understand what I was clearly seeing. *My daughter was not her anorexia.*

Of course, it's vital to call it what it is. Anorexia and other eating disorders can be life threatening. This isn't about denying that they exist and thereby becoming complicit with the eating disorder. This is about not attaching another label to their already fragile identity and sense of self.

I was truly seeing my daughter even when she couldn't see herself. I was seeing her, as Michael Neill, best-selling author and coach, so powerfully puts it, *"as the creative potential of the entire universe"*. That was my role. It was to see her potential, her character, her accomplishments, her beauty, her being, her relationships, her hobbies, her personality, and so much more. But all she was able to see was anorexia nervosa as who she was.

When we see that we're more than our thinking about who we are, we can be released from the prison we've created for ourselves. We don't have to be at war with ourselves.

"A man will be imprisoned in a room with a door that's unlocked and opens inwards as long as it does not occur to him to pull rather than push." ~ Ludwig Wittgenstein

Much like the man referred to in this quote, I was able to free myself from the thoughts about my identity as "the mum whose daughter has anorexia" simply by realising that this option was open to me. In releasing this, I was able to focus on healing myself, my attitude, my sense of self and let go of the fears around what others may or may not be thinking about me, Bea, and our family.

I refused to let anorexia be our family's identity.

21

WHO AM I IF NOT MY EATING DISORDER?

BEA

Over the last 10 years anorexia has been such a big part of my life that until recently it played a significant role in shaping how I saw myself as a person. For many years it defined me. It *was* me. I might as well have had it written on my business card.

I completely lost sight of the other parts of my life that make me who I really am. I went from *having* an eating disorder to *being* the eating disorder.

And to me, at the time, this wasn't something I saw as a bad thing. After all, I was good at it. I was good at being anorexic. When other things in my life weren't going so well, I knew that I could come top of the class at under-eating and over-exercising. There was a sense of pride that came with it too. I felt proud when I lost weight. I felt proud when I burned off more calories than I consumed.

I clung onto this identify because it was comfortable. Ironically, it felt safe. And when you become this comfortable, whatever it is you're getting comfortable with, it's hard to let it go.

You start to ask yourself the question "Who am I if not [insert noun]?" because you don't know what would fill its place if you weren't 'being' that person or playing that role.

But the thing is, you don't need to fill its place. You can let go of the labels and roles you've taken on or others have assigned to you and still be okay. We attach so much meaning to labels, whether it's 'mother', 'sister', 'girlfriend', or in my case 'anorexia sufferer'. But they don't need to define us.

If I think of my identity as a pie chart, when I was ill my eating disorder took up 100%. There wasn't any room left for the real me. What I realise now is that the only thing that was holding me back from letting go of this was my own thinking, which went something along the lines of:

- "This is the only thing I'm good at."
- "I'm not capable of doing anything else."
- "Giving up means I've failed."
- "How will they know I'm not okay if I give it up"?

It goes on...

But no one ever told me these things. I was the only one telling myself that I would be lost without my eating disorder. I believed the self-limiting stories that I was telling myself so that I would stay in the comfort zone of my illness.

But all we have to do to break out of this is to realise that our experience of life is created through our thinking. That's it.

And when we realise that, we can start to question and challenge the stories and see that they're not based on anything other than the thoughts running through our mind. When we do that we can see that we don't have to believe them. And that changes everything.

So if I were now to ask myself the question "Who am I if not my eating disorder?", I would say that I am whoever I want to be. I'm a sister, a daughter, a girlfriend, a budding photographer, a writer, and the list goes on.

Because when we understand how the mind works we are no longer limited by the unhelpful voices in our head telling us what we can or can't do or who we can or can't be.

Simply by recognising that we have the power to choose whether or not to believe the stories that are shaping our identity, we can see that there's no effort involved. We're not using different strategies and techniques to try and change how we view ourselves or how we feel; we are just able to know to take our thinking a little less seriously.

If you're wondering how you identify which thoughts you should or shouldn't trust, the way they make you feel is a good indicator of whether or not they're being helpful. For example, just the other day I had a whole lot of thinking about how terrible I was at my job. It made me feel pretty negative about myself. But then I reminded myself that I didn't have to believe it — so I didn't. Don't get me wrong, our minds can make pretty convincing arguments for why we should feel bad about ourselves. It therefore doesn't always feel like it can be that easy to dismiss or challenge negative thoughts, but I promise you it is. It just takes a bit of practice and after a while it will become second nature.

I'll admit, it did take me a while to get to a place where I didn't feel I had to buy into the identity I would regularly create for myself. The way I see identity now is completely different to how I saw it then. Before, I defined myself by the labels I was assigned: anorexic; high achiever; perfectionist. Identity was fixed. Once I had been branded, that was it, I was stuck with it.

Now I see identity as transient and flexible. It's ever-changing, and actually something I can have some fun with. Today I might choose to be a scruffy, flip-flop wearing tomboy; tomorrow I may choose to be a smartly dressed, feminine professional. It's a bit like delving into the dressing up box I had as a child. Each day and in every moment, I can choose what version of myself I want to be, and the only person who can change that is me.

22

DROPPING THE LABELS

REBECCA

I've got a bit of a love/hate relationship with labelling. We welcome labelling on food because it lets us know the ingredients, the use-by date, and cooking suggestions. We welcome labelling on clothing because it lets us know the fabric, size, and where it was made. In a way, I welcomed Bea's diagnosis at the time because it gave me a framework, it reassured me in some bizarre way that there was now something we could work with. Doctors and health professionals need a label, a diagnosis, so that they can put a plan together to heal their patients.

However, labels are used far too freely in my opinion and serve only to box us in to a diagnosis, a condition, a personality, whatever that might be. Here are some of the issues we can face with labelling:

- We run the risk of becoming a victim to our label
- We spend our life living up to our label
- We refuse to or don't risk breaking out of the label
- We see safety in the label

- We inadvertently give power to the label, which then keeps us trapped
- We get stuck in the label and become helpless
- We come to believe that all we are is our label or our diagnosis
- We end up letting go of all self-responsibility as we slide into becoming our label

So many of our beliefs about ourselves are keeping us boxed into a small life. Someone's fear of flying, or anxiety, or that they see themselves as shy are thoughts brought to life and seen as true. How many of them are actually true?

We think it's who we are. We limit ourselves, we trap ourselves into a small world and tell ourselves we're okay with that.

But what is a label anyway? A label, like any belief, is simply a thought. It's absolutely not who we are. Sure, we may have anxious thinking, we may get nervous before flying or public speaking, we may well have had a bad date or two... but it doesn't need to define us.

There's something I'd love you to do right now. Grab yourself a notebook and pen and open to a new page. Write these words: "I'm the sort of person who..." I'd like you to fill in the blank. You might actually simply prefer to write the words, "I am ..." and fill in that blank. Whichever you choose, I'd love you to write as many words you can think of to finish this sentence. No judgments, no second guessing, no crossing out, no considering in your head whether to write it down or not... write them all down.

The second half of this exercise is to ask yourself how much of what you've written is actually true. It might be good to work together with someone on this, or you might prefer to do it alone. Allow the truth to come to the surface.

There is extraordinary freedom to be found when we are able to see through the labels we have given ourselves and let them go. When we see that they aren't real, that we innocently created them as a way to make sense of our world, we are free to let them go.

23

THE PERFECTIONISM MIRAGE

BEA

I have always been told that when I was younger, I'd only ever do something if I knew I could do it well. When I was at walking age, I didn't stand up, fall over, and try again. I stood up and I walked.

I was like this through school as well: always in the top set, always worried about doing well. I was the ultimate perfectionist. And this manifested itself in all aspects of my life. So when I was diagnosed with anorexia, I felt that I had to be the best – that I had to strive for 'perfect'.

I don't think I quite knew what 'perfect' was but I knew that it was always thinner than what looked back at me in the mirror. But the goal posts were always moving. As soon as I reached what I originally thought was my target weight, my goal would instantly move. It was like chasing a mirage in the desert.

This is where the danger lies. I was chasing something that was always just out of reach, so I was never satisfied. It subsequently led to a whole whirlwind of thinking about how I was a failure and I wasn't good enough.

This can happen in all aspects of life. We so often say to ourselves "I'll be happy when…". But when we reach that goal, we've already moved onto the next thing that we think will make our lives complete.

It's a pretty unfair game if you think about it. Imagine running the 100m sprint at the Olympics and as you approach the finish line you're told that the distance has been changed to 200m. And then as you're getting ready to cross the line again it moves to 400m. You'd get pretty fed up, wouldn't you?

It makes you wonder why we do this to ourselves.

But what I'm coming to realise is that 'perfect' is a complete illusion. And it's not that we're just setting the bar that little bit too high. The bar doesn't exist. It's a figment of our imagination. How often have you thought to yourself "I'll be happy when I've achieved X", "I'll be successful when I have Y", but when you reach that point, the bar has already vanished and moved elsewhere?

When I had anorexia, my whole world was about chasing the mirage. But what I didn't realise at the time was that this thought-created illusion of an end point wouldn't make me feel happy or safe or content. Because life doesn't work like that. As we've said throughout this book, nothing 'out there' can shape our experience of life. It's what we think about what's 'out there' that makes us feel a certain way.

To use an example, some days when I was suffering from anorexia, I would feel totally fine with eating a particular snack, but on others I would feel physically sick at the thought of it. The snack hasn't changed. It was exactly the same as it was on the days when I would eat it. The difference is that my thinking about it had changed.

So, if we return to the idea of the perfectionism mirage, we all have our own beliefs about what perfect is; we all have our own bars that we set and then move. But despite the differences in content, they're all made of the same stuff — thought. And yet how much time and energy do we waste worrying about reaching our self-defined idea of perfect? Probably a bit too much.

24

INSECURITY AND IDENTITY

REBECCA

S ydney Banks (the man whose insights into the nature of the human experience we're sharing with you) was having a conversation with a colleague, and Syd told him that he felt insecure. His colleague responded by saying, "You're not insecure, Syd, you just *think* you are." Syd heard that response at a very deep level. He saw the extraordinary role that thought plays in our experience of life.

The dictionary defines 'insecure' with these words: subject to fears and doubts, not self-confident or assured, uneasy, and anxious.

I'm sure we've all felt insecure at times; many of us feel insecure a lot of the time. When we are feeling insecure we're in a low state of mind, and when we're in a low state of mind it feels like we're living out a storm in our heads.

Fortunately, once Bea and I understood where our experience of life was coming from, 100% of the time it's from within us, we didn't need to be so reactive and scared of our feelings. Don't get me wrong, we still have moments, and sometimes longer, of feeling insecure (we're human after all), but we take them less seriously now.

When you think that your experience is coming from outside — the relationship, the boss, the exam, the friend, the food — then it's understandable that you will feel insecure and threatened by life. When you see for yourself that your experience is created through your own thinking, then insecurity doesn't have the weight and meaning that it did before. We can unburden ourselves from our thoughts, and our feelings don't seem so life threatening anymore.

I think you'll agree that we're all looking for a good feeling. We're looking to feel better. What seems hard to grasp is that this feeling of wellbeing is always available to us. It's something we both heard said often when we came across this understanding. But when I was feeling bad, it was easy to question this truth. At times I wasn't able to see my or Bea's wellbeing.

Sometimes the insecurity feels so intense that we look outside for the solution to feeling better and reach for alcohol, or drugs, or restricting behaviours to bring us that 'good' feeling. At the time it really does feel like the solution. And perhaps for a moment it does bring solace and relief. The truth is that this feeling doesn't last forever and we end up feeling worse. We think we have to work harder, or drink more, or restrict more to get that feeling. It's never going to work that way round. We will be chasing the good feeling forever and never find it if we continue to look outside of ourselves.

When we see for ourselves that insecurity is only ever in our thinking, then reaching for our 'addiction' will no longer make sense. This is what I've seen in a number of areas in my life and Bea has seen so profoundly in her relationship with food. When I realised that opening the fridge at 6 p.m. and pouring a glass of wine wasn't the solution to my low mood, I stopped relying on it to make me feel better. It might have made me feel relaxed for a few moments, but I was back feeling anxious almost immediately.

When we feel secure we have much clearer thinking; we are in a very different state of mind and as a result are much more likely to make different choices for ourselves. We see through the illusion of our thinking and wouldn't dream of harming ourselves. It's much more fun to hang out in this place. We see and experience our potential and our creativity. From a secure place life looks and is much more enjoyable and easy. The secure place is our default setting, it's the blue sky that is always behind the clouds. The moment you see this, life looks very different and so much more hopeful.

SECTION 4: RELATIONSHIPS

"A deep sense of love and belonging is an irreducible need of all people. We are biologically, cognitively, physically, and spiritually wired to love, to be loved, and to belong."
~ Brené Brown

Something seems to happen in our early years that distorts how life really works and sets many of us on a path of disconnection and fear. We begin to look to the outside world for love, endorsement, recognition, approval, permission, and acceptance. We long for love and belonging without realising that we already have it. We are all connected. It is who we are. It is what we are. We are connected with you right now and we are holding a space for you, a space filled with love, care, and compassion.

Brené Brown sums this up so beautifully in the quote above. A deep sense of love and belonging is what we all desire, even if we don't realise it. It is all we ever want. It's what the pre-teen struggling with being bullied wants, it's what the

CEO of a giant corporation wants. It's what our politicians, nurses, farmers, students, lawyers, bus drivers, care workers, pop stars, elderly, rugby players, shopkeepers want.

For many of us it becomes a hard struggle to feel this love and connection either with ourselves or with others. As a result, relationships become difficult, we feel alone, we become isolated. We struggle to connect, we hide away in fear of being rejected, we feel incredibly vulnerable and we end up shutting down. We have both done it. We know others who have done it and continue to do so. There is a feeling and belief that it's safer to be an island, to be alone, because the fear to reach out, to connect, to show vulnerability, is too much of a risk to take. This is often when we turn to substances, to food, to alcohol, to self-harm, in the hope and with the belief that we'll feel less pain.

What we've forgotten, what has become hidden from view, is that we are loving beings and we are naturally connected to each other. Love and connection is our default; it's how we began life after all.

"Love is the secret ingredient. The ultimate superfood." - Kute Blackson

We came across this quote randomly and it seems perfectly apt right here. Love is always the answer. On the surface it looks like eating disorders are about food and that's maybe what people don't understand. Eating disorders are not about food — this is something Bea spoke a lot about at the time. The relationship is not with food, the relationship is with our thinking. Insecure thinking is the cause and the eating disorder is the byproduct used to manage what turns out to be unreliable thinking.

Whilst you read this section consider these three things:

- Who is in your support system?
- Notice where and when you feel most connected
- Consider that love is the secret ingredient

ME, MYSELF AND I... AND EVERYONE ELSE

BEA

When I had anorexia, it very much felt that it was me and Mum (and our somewhat complicated relationship) at the centre of my world, with everyone and everything else falling outside of that bubble. If I'm totally honest, I don't remember much about the rest of my family or the relationships I had with them at that time. I think everyone felt like they were walking on eggshells when they were around me, like I was a ticking time bomb that required careful handling. Inevitably, this led to an underlying feeling of tension at home, at school, or pretty much anywhere where I had to interact with people. It wasn't pleasant for anyone.

Back then we would always eat dinner together as a family. That had always been important to us and I have fond memories of us all sat around the kitchen table together. But when I was ill the atmosphere inevitably changed and I remember dinnertime becoming an extremely painful experience for everyone. What mood would I be in? Would I eat? Had Mum cooked the right thing? These are the sorts of questions I imagine were on everyone's minds. It was tense. But outside of mealtimes it felt like it was just me and Mum. This isn't to say that my Dad, brothers, and other members of the family weren't involved or didn't provide support - far from it. But for some reason, perhaps due to its intensity, the relationship I had with Mum seems to have stuck the most in my mind.

Our relationship felt almost bipolar at times. It was like we were either fighting each other or fighting my illness. One minute she was the enemy, making me eat and follow my meal plan; the next she was my safety net, catching me when I had no fight left in me. It must have been impossible for Mum or anyone for that matter

to know how to act around me. Should she be the strict parent who refuses to take any of my crap, or should she be the loving, caring mother who shows me nothing but love? Somehow she managed to balance the two.

I resented her having to be the strict parent, but really she didn't have a choice. If she hadn't done everything she could to keep me on track with my eating, I have no doubt that I would have become much more ill than I did. And while I may not remember much about the role my wider family played at that time, I know that having them there was hugely important. They were a vital support system, even if I didn't realise it at the time.

While my relationship with Mum was volatile, for want of a better word, looking back I see how important it is for family members to be able confront the illness and not pussy foot around it so much. While it may be painful and exhausting at the time, having someone play the 'bad guy' is the only way to challenge the illness. To say this added fuel to an already fiery relationship is an understatement, but Mum wasn't (or didn't seem) afraid to stand her ground. She wasn't going to be bullied into submission, and I think that made all the difference in the long run. Certainly now it means we have an extraordinarily strong relationship.

What I can see now is that while it may have seemed that what Mum said or did would cause me to respond or behave in a certain way, such as restricting my food intake, that wasn't actually the case. Her words or actions would trigger me to think, but they can't make me *do* anything. My mind interprets what she has said, drawing on past experiences to help it decide how to respond, and at the same time creates a feeling and emotion to match. Usually this went something like:

Mum: "Bea, you ate that very quickly, do you want some more?"

Bea: "No."

Bea's thoughts: "I wish she would stop commenting on how much I eat! I've clearly eaten too much."

Bea's feelings: Anger and resentment.

But the great thing about knowing that our feelings are created from thought is that it gives us the freedom to react and respond in different ways to what may seem like the same situation or 'trigger'. So now if that conversation happened today it might go something like:

Mum: "Bea, you ate that very quickly, do you want some more?"

Bea: "No thanks, but I was clearly hungry!"

Bea's thoughts: "That meal was great, but I'm stuffed!"

Bea's feelings: Full and content.

While these two conversations may have taken place almost a decade apart, nothing about me (or Mum) has really changed. We are still the same people, it's just that now our understanding of our thinking is very different to what it was 10 years ago.

During this time, I have seen how what is said between two people (and what is read between the lines) can so often make or break a relationship. We interpret things differently to how they were intended. We get the wrong end of the stick. But it doesn't have to be that way. We all have the incredible capability to make up elaborate and very convincing stories about what we think someone *really* meant when they said something. We take these stories as fact when in reality they are based on nothing more than our own thoughts and beliefs.

This ability we have is a double-edged sword though, so we must learn to use it responsibly. I could make up and believe a story about how I'm an introvert who is terrible at speaking in public, or I could believe that I am brilliant public speaker who occasionally let's her anxious thinking get the better of her. Both stories are created in the exact same way, they're made of the same stuff, but it's down to us which one we choose to believe.

26

STAY OUT OF THE BOXING RING

REBECCA

One of the things that kept me awake at night when Bea was ill was my relationship with her and the anorexia. I wanted to show the eating disorder that I wasn't scared of it whilst showing Bea nothing but unconditional love. But the anorexia was a wily, cunning beast and would draw me in, befriend me, and then before I knew it I was on the verge of becoming complicit with the anorexic behaviours.

When we as carers understand that our thinking creates our reality and that we are never responsible for how someone else thinks, feels, or sees the world, we can get on with looking after and loving them unconditionally.

I often use the metaphor of a boxing ring with my clients because it does feel like we're fighting a lot of the time. This is how I see it. It takes two people to be in the ring to fight. You can decide whether or not you want to be in the ring slugging it out. Is being in the ring really that helpful? Sometimes it takes a while for us to notice that we've climbed in there with them. The moment we realise this is what's happening we can get out.

I remember a time when Bea and I were fighting — emotions were high, words were flying around. I realised what was happening and said that I was going to leave the room. I didn't trust what was going to come out of my mouth next, and I just knew that it wouldn't be helpful. Bea was really angry with me for walking away. I left the room and went to my bedroom and sat there quietly whilst I gathered my thoughts and my state of mind naturally improved. Twenty minutes or so later I returned downstairs and we'd both calmed down and were able to have a much more helpful and loving conversation. Choosing to leave the boxing ring I'm sure saved us on many occasions.

When I stopped feeling guilty, and somehow responsible, for Bea's moods, I was able to get on with my life and being the best support and guide for her and her brothers. Even when someone is telling you, pointing at you, angry with you and shrieking that it's your fault that they feel a certain way, it's really never your fault.

The times you find yourself in a calm space with a quiet mind, you'll find your sense of serenity quite appealing to others; it affects others around you. They will feel naturally drawn towards your peace and it helps them to relax, to unwind and perhaps to breathe a little slower. There would be times when I was in a good place and Bea would come up to me and curl up on the sofa with me or ask to come out on a dog walk and lovingly put her arm through mine as we walked along the road in companionable silence. From this place of stillness, solutions become visible, relationships become much more harmonious and loving. We are much more able to feel compassion for someone else when we have a clearer mind.

We are able to relax much more easily when we recognise that it is our thinking that is the cause of our suffering, not anyone or anything out there.

Living my life and keeping as normal a life as possible for the family was important. If we all focussed on the anorexia (which we did a lot of the time) then we all ended up in low states of mind, in and out of the boxing ring. There was resentment, anger, confusion, frustration, all because we were being sucked into this low state of mind because of our own personal thinking getting the better of us. It is always insecure thinking that pulls us into a low state of mind. Compassion and love brings us out of it. It's always wise to stay out of the boxing ring.

27

STOP POINTING THE FINGER

BEA

arlier in this section I wrote about how someone's actions or words can't actually make you react or behave in a particular way. What's actually happening is that their actions trigger you to think, which in turn (often instantaneously) produces feelings which we react on. So we're never reacting to what they've actually said or done, rather we're reacting to our own thinking and feelings. I'm not trying to say that this is a bad thing, far from it. What I'm trying to say is that by knowing how it works, it takes the power away from the other person.

If you think about it, have you ever reacted in a particular way to something that happened or was said and on another occasion you have reacted completely differently to the same thing? I know I have. The other day my boyfriend said something to me that I took really personally and this put me in a grump for the rest of the evening. Today he said the exact same thing and I didn't react at all. Funny, isn't it?

The good thing about this is that you don't have to feel like you're being held victim to someone else's words or actions.

This isn't to say that you're never going to get upset about anything ever again. It just means you can move past it much quicker.

However, what I initially found hard about choosing whether or not to take my thinking seriously, is realising I have to take more responsibility for my own feelings. It's much easier to point the finger and say that it's her fault that I did X, or he made me do Y. But what we should actually be doing is reflecting on whether we really need to take the thoughts in our head quite so seriously.

Pointing the finger is just an innocent misunderstanding. We all do it. But when we realise that we have more responsibility than we think, it can sometimes be a bitter pill to swallow.

This happened a lot when I was ill. In my mind, what Mum, the doctor, or anyone said or did directly caused me to feel a certain way. It was her fault that I felt upset. She made me feel angry and miserable. As you can imagine, this presented some challenges to our relationship, but that's how it looked to me at the time. When Mum would hover over me while I weighed out my cereal in the mornings, I would feel angry and resentful towards her. In my mind, it was her actions that were making me feel that way.

But at the time, I didn't realise that no one had the power to make me feel a certain way. Although if I'm totally honest, even if I had known this at the time, I think I still would have found it easier to continue blaming others for my misery and not take responsibility. Often, deep down, I didn't actually want to be happy, so maintaining this mindset made it pretty easy. Even today, when my boss says something irritating or the rain is lashing down around me and I just want to be a bit grumpy, it's so much easier to blame the person or the thing. But at the back of my mind I always know that it's never my boss or the rain that's really making me feel that way.

Pride also plays a role in this. Have you ever been really mad at someone and then you get to a point where you can't actually remember why you were mad at them in the first place? But instead of just dropping it and moving on, we stubbornly stay in that mood because we don't want to look stupid or like we've conceded. This happens so often when two people have an argument — no one wants to be the first to back down and apologise because our pride (which is just made up thinking anyway) gets in the way. We would all save ourselves so much pain and suffering if we dropped our pride once in a while and allowed ourselves to bounce back to our default setting of being at peace.

28

WE'RE ALL DOING THE BEST WE CAN

REBECCA

"Everyone is doing the best they can given the thinking they have that looks real to them."
~ *Sydney Banks*

These words from Syd Banks are the ones that resonate the most with me, and each time I read them I find my shoulders drop and relax a little more. Perhaps you too can let out a sigh or feel a little relief wash over you knowing that we're all doing the best we can, even when we think otherwise.

Somewhere deep inside I did know this back then but perhaps didn't want to believe it. On the surface I continued with the self-judgment and continued to blame myself. There were days that I wanted to take these feelings out on Bea and shout, 'Just eat, please, for heaven's sake'. So many around me were asking me:

"Why doesn't she just eat for goodness sake?"

She really was doing the best she could given the thinking

that was very real for her. Food, as Bea has said, had become her enemy. How powerful our minds are. How powerful that they can trick us in such a convincing and destructive way.

In a way, my mind was doing a similar thing. I was starting to believe that somehow it was my fault. This too was simply my thinking, and it was not serving me well at the time. But there were times that it looked so real, so convincing. It looked like it was the unhappiness in my life, the unhappiness in my marriage that was causing Bea to not eat, especially when her weight plummeted when her father and I separated. My identity was in danger of becoming wrapped up in the role of carer, someone who couldn't help their child to be well, as well as someone with a failing marriage. If only I'd been able to see, even just for a few moments, that I was doing the best I could at the time.

And what of my sons, my darling boys? I struggled to see that I was doing the best I could. Ollie was preparing for university at the time of Bea's illness, he was taking the next steps in his life. How was he doing? Was he struggling? I don't think I ever asked him. It was too painful to talk about and I buried so many feelings. I was making up stories about my own ability to be the best mum for ALL my children. I was scared the boys would turn their backs on me. I was scared of failure.

Let's take a moment to stop and reflect. Do you see that it's not actually possible to cause someone to feel something? Nothing I do or say can actually cause you to feel an emotion. Nothing you do or say can cause a shift in my emotions. The only thing that brings about a shift in my feelings or emotions is *my* thinking. It was my thinking about my circumstances that caused me to feel the way I did, and it was unhelpful, yet at the same time so very mesmerising. My thinking was leading me to believe that if I somehow took the blame for Bea's illness it might ease her suffering.

It's the words "...with the thinking they have that looks real to them" in Syd Banks' quote above that touch me deeply. This is what sets us free. When we see this we are liberated from what's holding us back. We experience a deeper grace and compassion.

We are never out to deliberately hurt ourselves or others, even when we take part in self-harm, denying ourselves nourishment, bingeing, purging, or abusing alcohol or drugs. It simply seems like the best and only course of action at the time as a way to free ourselves from the pain we're experiencing. It feels like the relief we need. And for a moment it really looks like it brings us that relief.

When we see that we are doing the best we can, and that others too are doing the best they can, we are free to forgive, to have compassion, to love freely and whole-heartedly.

Our head wants us to figure it out, to think our way to a solution, yet this isn't the way to find the answer. The answer lies in connecting with our heart. From this place of deep connection we're much more able to understand that they are where they are, wrapped up in their suffering, because of what they are thinking. Our role here is to point them in a more helpful direction, to understand that they do not have to take that thinking seriously. This new direction enables them (and us) to see that we've created our experience via the extraordinary power of thought.

"Thought creates our world, and then says, 'I didn't do it'." ~
David Bohn, theoretical physicist

What do you hear in this quote? I was baffled by it the first
time I read it. I wasn't sure I really understood it. What does
it mean, "I didn't do it"? And then one day I understood it. I
realised it was like drawing a picture of a monster, a spider,
or a snake, pinning it to the wall, forgetting I drew it and
then each time I walked past it screaming in fear. It doesn't
make sense, does it? Yet we're doing this every moment of
our lives. We're having fear-based thoughts, and seeing and
believing them as if they are true, forgetting that we're the
ones who created them in the first place.

Bea had developed fear-based thoughts around eating, body
image and self-awareness. Nobody had planted those
thoughts in her head; she'd inadvertently sowed the seeds
that food was the enemy and then she believed them.

This is where true healing lies — seeing through the illusion that we've created.

We can't create good feelings from a fear-based place. We
can't feel good when we believe thoughts that are grounded
in fear.

This is not about managing and controlling our thoughts.
We can't ever do that, no matter what anyone tries to tell
you. We have no control whatsoever over the content of our
thinking. What we can decide is which thoughts to bring to
life and which to let pass. Thoughts are temporary, they are
transient, they're like steam rising from a pan of boiling
water, here one moment and gone the next.

Thought is the source of all our experience, it is not reality,
yet we make it so and get caught up in it as if it were real. I

like to think of it like a hologram. Our thinking creates something that looks three dimensional in the moment and yet it's not; it vanishes on closer inspection. It's not something we can hold in our hand and yet we live our lives as if it were real.

Our child, or whoever it is we care for, has an eating disorder because of thinking that seems so real to them that they act on it and develop the habits that result in them suffering. Whatever language they use when they are in the throes of an episode or period of time is not who they are.

The image of the girl looking in the mirror and seeing herself as overweight when we look at her and see someone who is starving; the young man who doesn't believe he is talented and yet we as the observer see his extraordinary gift; the musician who only sees her faults; the parent who only sees themselves through the eyes of the last time they yelled at their child... thoughts create these illusions.

It affects us all. All the time. And it's all an illusion.

We're all doing the best we can even when we can't see it. Even when we think or believe we should be better or know what to do, even after we've exhausted our list, even then, we are still doing the best we can with the thinking that looks so real to us.

Once we realise this we can let go, or even simply let it be. Knowing and understanding this helped me to radically heal the past.

29

CUTTING MYSELF OFF FROM THE OUTSIDE WORLD

BEA

As I mentioned earlier in the book, I don't remember much about the relationships I had with my friends or family when I was ill. The very nature of being caught up in my thinking all the time meant that I didn't have the mental capacity or the will to create and maintain any meaningful relationships. So I cut myself off, I stopped making an effort, and I became very isolated.

As a result, I became even more focused on what was going on in my own head. It's hardly surprising that the more attention I gave my thinking, the more real and all-consuming it became. I ended up becoming my own best friend and my worst enemy at the same time.

I was the only one who could understand what I was thinking and how I was feeling. This caused me to become very protective and even territorial of my illness. A girl at school once asked me for tips on how to become anorexic (as you can guess, we didn't speak much after that). Not only was I completely outraged at her insensitivity, I also felt like she was asking for me to reveal my deepest secret. I didn't want her to be anorexic, not just because it's a horrible thing to wish upon anyone, but because it was my domain. I was good at it and I didn't want anyone else to steal the limelight, so I distanced myself from her and others so I didn't feel threatened. Despite the suffering, my distorted thinking made me want to cling on to the very thing that was causing me so much pain.

Throughout my time at school I found myself on the edge of friendship groups. I've never been someone who thrives or even enjoys being part of a big group — I would choose an evening at the pub with my closest friends over a house party any day. Maybe this is due to a lack of confidence or simply just my preference, I don't know. But when I was ill I was so preoccupied that I was never able to throw myself fully into the friendships I had. It left me feeling very isolated.

I was withdrawing from what I thought were the threats of the outside world. I didn't trust anyone, so to me it made sense to disengage from those around me. I very much saw life as something that was happening to me. Eating made me anxious; the doctors made me resentful; exercising gave a sense of achievement. I felt totally out of control when it came to how I was feeling so would do more of the things that I believed would make me feel better, like restricting my food intake and over-exercising. I saw my feelings and emotions as a product of what I was doing or what was going on around me. I never picked up on the fact that the feeling I got from those things wasn't always consistent. Sometimes an hour in the gym would make me feel on top of the world; sometimes it would leave me full of self-loathing. Sometimes eating a piece of toast would make me physically sick; sometimes I actually enjoyed it.

So the idea that what happens 'out there' has the ability to make us feel a certain way just doesn't stack up. It's refreshing to know now that life doesn't work that way. Nothing, other than the thoughts in my head, can make me feel anything. External circumstances can trigger me to think, but they cannot dictate the feeling or emotion that those thoughts in turn create.

This means we are no longer at the mercy of other people's words or actions (and we never were in the first place). It means that I don't have to respond to something in a prede-termined manner, like feeling anxious when I have to choose what to eat at a restaurant, or closing off when someone talks to me about eating disorders. The only thing that is causing me to feel that way are the thoughts running through my mind in that moment.

Those thoughts may draw on past experience and old memories to determine the feeling it produces, but knowing that it's not the thing (the menu, the conversation, whatever it is) that is causing me to feel a certain way opens us up to a whole world of possibilities. A world where going to a restaurant can be exciting, not scary. A world where I can talk about eating disorders all day long and not feel any different than if I were discussing the weather. So while cutting myself off from the outside world seemed like a sensible thing to do at the time, I know now that there was never anything 'out there' that I needed to hide from in the first place.

30

SEPARATE REALITIES

REBECCA

"Reality is an illusion, albeit a very persistent one."
~ *Albert Einstein*

Every single one of the 7.6 billion people on this planet has a different reality, a totally different experience of life. What we think of as reality is just *our* experience of *our* life. Speak to grown up siblings about their experience of growing up and each will have a completely different story of home life. Sometimes it feels like they weren't actually raised by the same parents! My sister and I had a conversation recently about something that happened when we were children and we both had completely different memories of it. I'd carried it as a burden for years and she hadn't given it a moment's thought. Crazy isn't it? I'm sure you've got similar stories. None of them right, none of them wrong, all simply *our* experience of *our* reality.

Ask a handful of people who have just come out of the cinema and each one will have had a different experience.

My son and I watched the Oscar-winning film Moonlight at the cinema one evening; as the credits rolled we looked at each other overwhelmed and speechless at the beauty, subtlety and sensitivity of the film. A woman in front of us stood up, turned to her partner and said, "Well, that's two hours of my life I'll never get back."

Separate realities.

The truth of separate realities really comes home to me when I think about people's very individual music taste. My partner enjoys listening to rap and R&B. He listens to BBC Radio 1xtra. I enjoy classical music, acoustic guitar, reggae, the old soul classics, and jazz. I really do dislike his music! He loves it. He doesn't see what I enjoy about listening to classical music. Bea's boyfriend loves watching and playing football... she doesn't.

Separate realities!

And a lot of the time we believe our reality is the right one. We've probably never considered it to be otherwise. What if this wasn't the case?

What I think and believe about myself isn't necessarily true either; it's just a version of me. What you, my partner, my children, and my parents think of me is all very different and all of it is created in our own version of reality.

What if we could take some time to walk in someone else's shoes or look at life through their eyes? How different would our experiences be? How different would our relationships be?

I remember an exercise we did when I was training to be a coach, which was at the time Bea was ill. We had to choose a partner and then go for a walk, one in front of the other. The person following had to copy exactly how the leader walked, their pace, their stride, how they moved their arms, their body, their head. After 10 minutes we swapped. It was interesting to walk in someone else's shoes for a while. The woman I was partnered with had a wonderful relaxed way of walking, she seemed totally comfortable and at ease in life — that was the feeling I got. I told her this and she agreed. I, on the other hand was told that my walk was fast and intense; she felt she'd had a workout and felt quite short of breath once we'd finished. She said she felt quite anxious. Yes, that was about right, that's exactly how it felt for me too. That was my life at the time.

If we can see that our version of reality is just that, it's ours, it's not someone else's, then we open ourselves up to seeing much more. What could I have seen in Bea that might have helped me understand her a little more? What could she have seen from where I was standing that might have led her to question her own beliefs about herself?

We can use our differences as the source of discord in our relationships or we can enjoy the differences, we can become intrigued by others' interests, beliefs and reality. When we get quiet and listen to the other person, we learn from them. When we take the time to understand and connect rather than insist on being 'right' we open up the way for real listening, understanding, and compassion. And this puts us on the path to healing.

There is such freedom when we see that we can decide to not take our reality so seriously, we can treat it lightly and even question the truth of it. What of our own private battles with ourselves when we see through the illusion, when we see the stories we've created about ourselves and how real they look? What of our 'battles' with friends, family, and the wider world? Reconciliation always begins with ourselves, finding the space for self-acceptance, for self-forgiveness, for self-love. Remember that we're all doing the best we can given the version of reality we're seeing. What if we were to put on different glasses and see something completely differently?

PROTECTING AND MANIPULATING

BEA

I have always wanted to look after other people. At school I was seen as the mum of our friendship group, always making sure everyone was okay. In my friendships now, I hate to see anyone upset or hurt, so I'll do anything I can to support them and help them to feel better.

This maternal instinct took on a new form when I had anorexia. I became a feeder. I've always loved to cook and bake, it's what I grew up doing, and that didn't change when I was ill. What did change was that I wouldn't eat any of the food I created. I would make mountains of brownies or boxes of cookies for those around me. I would make sure that everyone apart from me was well fed. Yet the most I would ever eat was a lick of the batter from the bowl before it went into the dishwasher.

I was totally obsessed with food and everything about it, but I managed to get my fix through cooking, watching endless cookery programmes and pouring over the pictures in recipe books. I was absorbing the food through my other senses so didn't feel the need to eat it.

I used to and still do share a love of cooking with my younger brother, Dan. We used to bake chocolate brownies together when we were younger and still today make a great team in the kitchen. But I was worried that he would pick up my bad habits when he would see me eat nothing more than a crumb of what we made together. So I would make excuses or even pretend to eat it so he and others wouldn't ask questions.

But cooking was more than just a way for me to satisfy my desperate need for food; it was a way of protecting other people. I felt responsible for making sure everyone else was well nourished. In my mind, I was protecting them from anorexia. I became increasingly aware of what other people were eating and would often worry if I thought they hadn't eaten enough and would encourage them to eat more. I was doing what other people were doing to me, I just couldn't seem to practice what I preached.

This behaviour continued for a long time and to an extent it still exists. I still love to cook for other people; I will still notice if someone isn't eating enough. The difference now is that I will actually eat what I cook and I won't worry so much about what other people are eating.

But on the flip side of my protective, maternal behaviour was the way I would manipulate relationships in order to get my way. I would use the trust that I had built up with someone to get away with not eating. At school I would spend a lot of time with the nurse who was tasked with monitoring me while I ate my lunch. It was a torturous process, but after a while she trusted me enough to eat in the next room by myself while she treated other patients. But I exploited the trust she placed in me. When I was left alone I would pour my smoothie down the sink and throw my food away. Writing about it now makes me sound like a nasty person, but at the time it felt like the right thing to do. I felt that I had to do anything I could to beat the system.

The ease with which I would switch from being the protector to the manipulator goes to show how easily we can move from thought to thought and 'become' different people. I don't think I made a conscious choice to assume these different roles. To me it just felt instinctive to try and protect the people I love and to manipulate those who stood in the way of me achieving my goals.

But I can now see that nothing I do can protect people from the outside world, or indeed their thinking about the outside world. Everyone already has everything they need to be happy and healthy — nothing I do will change that. And when it comes to manipulation, I now see that the only person I was really hurting was myself. I was so caught up in trying to play the system that I lost sight of the fact that the only one playing that game was me, and I was losing.

SECTION 5: INNATE WELLBEING

"Mental health lies within the consciousness of all human beings, but it is shrouded and held prisoner by our own erroneous thoughts." ~ Sydney Banks

In 2016 we came across a new psychology, a radical understanding of how the mind works. It changed everything for us and proved to be the 'missing link' in Bea's recovery. It's an understanding that has gone by a number of names: The Three Principles, Innate Health, Health Realization, and the Inside Out Understanding.

A Scottish man by the name of Sydney Banks saw something in the words, "you're not insecure Syd, you just think you are" that went way beyond the simple sentence uttered by a fellow attendee at a workshop in the early 1970s. What Syd saw led him to uncover what is being seen as a paradigm shift in psychology and is now rapidly spreading throughout the world. This understanding is opening the eyes, hearts, and minds of people across all sectors, including business, education, prisons, community, and mental health services, as well as sports psychology.

Syd's articulation of the Three Principles points us to how the mind works. The Principles, as we refer to them, are not prescriptive; they don't tell us how to live. They're also not another set of techniques to add to the self-help tool box. The Principles simply describe how life works for us as human beings whatever our creed, colour, age, gender, whatever life has dealt us, wherever we've been and wherever we're going. We experience life through the Three Principles whether we realise it or not.

32

THE THREE PRINCIPLES IN BRIEF

REBECCA

The Principle of Mind, simply put, makes all life possible. We are alive. It's our power source. It's the invisible intelligence that allows cuts to heal, our hearts to send blood around our bodies, the grass to grow, birds to migrate, bulbs to push through the earth in the Spring, planets to rotate in space without colliding — none of this is 'managed' by human beings, it simply happens without any input from us. If we leave nature to it, it knows what to do and, more often than not, does it better when we don't interfere!

Over the centuries many different groups, be they religious, spiritual or scientific, have tried to describe why this 'intelligence' is there, and as we know all too well, many of these groups disagree over their explanation! We have no comment to make about this. We are simply acknowledging that there is an intelligence present. When we tap into or fall back into this space, life just seems easier. We make decisions effortlessly, relationship problems seem to vanish, we feel more connected and purposeful, we feel more inspired and generally okay.

Michael Neill, speaking of the Principle of Mind in his book "The Inside Out Revolution" says, "In fact I've yet to meet anyone who hasn't at least some awareness of a part of themselves that exists beyond whatever personal trials and tribulations we all face. And the more time we spend connected with that part of ourselves, the more beautiful our life, and the impact of that life, becomes."

The Principle of Thought tells us that everything we experience in life comes from thought. Everything. It's hard to get our heads around that because we often don't see it as thought. We exist in a world of thought. It's like asking us what we think of gravity and how we manage it in our day to day lives, or asking the birds what they think about the air they fly in. It is such an intrinsic part of our lives that we don't realise its importance. Thought is the content of our lives. We have no control over thought; it flows through us enabling us to create the life we live.

All our beliefs and opinions are thoughts brought to life. Yet we aren't our thoughts; we don't actually need to take them seriously. In fact, life becomes easier when we take our thinking less seriously. Thought is like the potter's clay, with infinite possibilities of what we can create.

Sydney Banks puts it much more poetically: "Your thoughts are like the artist's brush, they create a personal picture of the reality you live in."

The Principle of Consciousness is the very fact that we are awake in life and have awareness. Consciousness brings our thoughts to life, allowing us to fully experience what it is to be alive. Whatever we think, we bring into life, in all its glory, through our feelings and emotions. You can't have a thought without an emotional experience of it.

Let's show you.

Close your eyes for a moment and take yourself for a walk on the beach, feel the sun on the back of your neck, the hot sand between your toes as you walk towards the glistening turquoise sea, smell the ocean and listen to the crashing waves. Can you feel the cool sea as it washes over your toes? How refreshing does that feel? Listen to the sound of the seagulls flying overhead. They're noisy aren't they!

Amazing isn't it? I bet you're not reading this by that ocean and yet you have been able to bring it to life. That's consciousness bringing your thoughts into action right there.

"We live in the feeling of our thinking. I liken it to the special effects department of the human system", Mara Gleason wrote in her book "One Thought Changes Everything".

The Three Principles simply describe how the human operating system works. They do not make judgments on how we should live. They just are. Just like gravity, which is experienced by every person no matter what. No one taught us how to apply gravity, it's just there. It's the same with the Principles.

33

FINDING OUR WAY BACK HOME

REBECCA

"Every problem we have in life is the result of losing our bearings and getting caught up in the content of our thinking. The solution to every one of these problems is finding our way back home."
~ Michael Neill

I have tears in my eyes as I begin to write. These words by Michael Neill touch me so profoundly. I wish I'd known this at so many times in my life when I felt I was lost. The depression I suffered as a child, the years of postnatal depression and the dips in and out when I was struggling to make sense of things that were happening in my life in my 30s and 40s. The agonising pain I felt when Bea was sick, all these times I wish I'd known what I now know. I had simply lost my bearings.

And yet it's funny because even during those dark times, there were moments when I felt a profound sense of peace in the quiet of my own stillness. How had I got there? What was I seeing and feeling there? I don't know how but I do know that it was based in a quiet mind. Peace came when I was free of my constant thoughts. It didn't always come in meditation or yoga, it didn't necessarily come on the walks on the beach when I was back at home in South Wales, perhaps it was when I was lying on my bed at the end of the day. Perhaps it was sitting quietly with a friend or even at times when I was surrounded with a lot of people and noise. In a way it doesn't matter how, what matters is that I found that peace. I now know that peace is something we all have access to, all the time. Every one of us, even if we don't believe we have.

That place of peace is what I refer to as 'home', not the bricks and mortar of home but some place within that is always there. It's always available, simply waiting for us to connect back in. It's the space within us all. We simply forget it exists when we get so caught up in the outside world, when it's begging us to look here or there or listen to this or that, when the outside world is calling our name louder and louder and more insistently. We end up thinking that we don't have wisdom, confidence, clarity, or peace of mind. We believe the answer is outside of us.

For years I thought 'home' was some place I could go and find. I thought I'd find it in the self-help books I devoured, the courses and workshops I attended, the videos from gurus I'd come to rely on. My shelves groaned with the weight of my search.

We've all lost our bearings at some stage or other and I'm guessing, given that this book is in your hands, you know what I mean. The answer doesn't lie with Bea, or with me, there are no how-tos in this book, as you'll have seen, it's not a step by step manual to recovery. We're simply the signpost pointing you back home.

I spent so many years caught up in the content of my thinking; I've come to believe most of us do. Believing and taking our thinking seriously is what causes our suffering. It is our thinking — or rather getting trapped in our thinking and the belief that it is reality — that brought us to this point of pain. It tells us so powerfully that we should listen to it. The louder it shouts, the stronger its opinions, the more we feel we have no choice but to comply, to listen, to take orders from it. We don't have to listen.

34

THE ILLUSION

REBECCA

"All we are is love, peace and wisdom and the power
to create the illusion that we're not." ~ Jack Pransky

We all live in a world of separate realities, as I shared with you in the previous section. It looks like life is happening 'out there', it looks like what I'm seeing with my eyes is reality, and we think that others are experiencing the exact same thing. On some level we know that this isn't true. A handful of people in a meeting will come out with very different thoughts about how productive, or otherwise, the meeting was. Rain in a dry, sun-baked country is a blessing, while in countries where the rain is incessant, the sun would be a blessing!

I would look at Bea and see a very thin girl who I longed to give a good meal to. When Bea looked at herself in the mirror, she didn't see a thin girl. She saw something that I didn't see. In a way we were both deluded in each other's eyes. A delusion is a false belief or opinion and this describes exactly what we were both seeing. Our realities were completely different. There would be no point yelling at her to eat because in her eyes food was the enemy and however ridiculous and incredible that seemed to me, and to her now, back then that was the 'reality' we were dealing with.

So if we're not experiencing 'reality', what is going on? What we are actually experiencing is a projection of our thinking. We have thoughts that pass through a series of filters, judgments, beliefs, past experiences, all in a fraction of a second. There's a beautiful quote that I've traced (correctly I hope) back to the Talmud: "We do not see things as they are, we see them as we are." This sums it up exactly.

We really never experience the world as it is, only as we are. Reality truly is subjective. In Bea's eyes food was something to be avoided at all costs; she was seeing that through her projector and it looked very real to her. She believed the thinking that she had at the time. We all do that. We see it as fact. The moment we wake up to the truth that we *have* thoughts rather than we *are* our thoughts, we begin to see through the illusion of what we've been creating. Until that point we are like the vast majority who are casualties in our own thought-created realities.

35

OUR FACTORY SETTINGS

REBECCA

W isdom, intuition, or gut feeling, this is our factory setting. It refers to our inner guidance system and is our natural state of being. Bea described it to me as being like the factory setting on a mobile phone or laptop. All runs smoothly and perfectly when we bring it home from the shop. All's good for a while but it's when we start adding apps, programmes, and keep tabs open that it slows it right down and the system then doesn't work as efficiently as it could. It's the same with us! The more 'noise' in our heads, the more tabs we have open, the less clearly we are able to see things.

When we realise that we don't have to take any notice of the constant chatter in our heads (which can admittedly feel utterly overwhelming at times) we get to experience calm, peace of mind, and serenity. Right now that might feel like a pipe dream, a fantasy, something way out of reach. We get that. We've both been in that place (and drop back there from time to time!) However, a quiet mind is available to all of us. It's a feeling we all know; it's just that many of us have forgotten what it's like. And because we've forgotten what it feels like, many of us go in search of 'the perfect quiet mind'. For others that search takes us to yoga, meditation, and silent retreats. We want to show you that a quiet mind is available to all of us, all the time, and that no search is necessary.

Let me explain how I see it. We're all looking for a beautiful feeling, serenity, or peace of mind. We go on an outward journey away from ourselves believing the answer lies out there. All the signs in the world point us out there, into the world, for the answer. You just need to spend a little time on Google to see the 'truth' in that.

We get caught in ever more extreme ways to end our suffering and find peace. We end up restricting or bingeing or self-harming because for a while it looks like it takes away the pain and we'll feel good. It's done innocently because we've forgotten that these good feelings lie within us; they did so from birth, yet we mistakenly started looking away from ourselves and towards the outside, to people, to things, to situations.

These things can't ever give us the peace that we're longing to reconnect with. We end up feeling more and more inse-cure, unloved, fragile, unhappy, and obsessive in our search outside for the answer. We don't think to look within us, especially when we're bombarded by the 'demands' of social media that leaves us feeling even more inadequate and insecure.

All we ever want is to feel good and feel happy. In fact, let me rephrase that, all we ever want is to feel okay. And yet when we're caught up in the storm of thought we feel anything but okay. Peace of mind feels a million miles away.

We have all felt that, and honestly there are days that we still feel that. The difference now is that we no longer take the thinking that moves us away from a quiet mind so seriously.

We appreciate that you might have a lot of thinking right now, perhaps some judgments. You might be thinking, "Yes, but you don't know my story, you don't know what it's like for me. I've never felt that feeling you describe. That's just not possible for me." The only thing we ask is that you keep reading and re-reading if necessary. Notice your thoughts and put them to one side as best you can. Let us metaphorically keep taking you by the hand and leading you to perhaps see something very different.

36

LETTING OUR INNER GPS DO THE WORK

REBECCA

We all have an inner GPS. I loved this idea when I first came across it when Michael Neill wrote, or spoke, about it in one of his podcasts. It's something that's preloaded into the human system, which I appreciate might sound a bit weird. It's always running and always correct. We refer to it by a number of different names — wisdom, intuition, inner knowing — you may have your own language for this. I like to think of it as a self-righting mechanism, like a lifeboat that rights itself even in the direst of weather conditions and circumstances.

Our inner GPS is always reliable, and it always has our best interests at heart. It's a feeling we get. We've all had it, we've all ignored it and we've all experienced that beautiful feeling when we've followed it. This is one of the things that we've said to each other, "Go with the good feeling". We believe this is where the answers lie. When we're in this good feeling, we're in a better state of mind and from this place we're much more likely to hear it guiding us along the right path.

Sounds great, doesn't it? The problem is that we don't always rely on our inner knowing. We think we have to work harder, to think more, to use our 'brain' to work things out. Trusting our inner GPS has become something we've lost touch with doing. We override it, and yet we know somewhere inside that we're doing that. We know when we're taking a left turn, when the GPS is telling us to go straight on. We know somewhere inside.

When we trust that our wisdom has our back, we can let go of so much of the heavy lifting, the hard work in life. It's just like having a navigation system in the car, when we trust that it knows the way to wherever we're going, we can let go of the worry about the intricate details. Our GPS has us covered. There's another great advantage when we trust our inner wisdom; when we realise that we don't need to have it all worked out in advance, we're then freer to enjoy the ride of life.

We've no idea in advance how a conversation will go, what's going to be on the exam paper or how the interview will turn out. We've no idea whether we'll win the prize or get the first class degree or whatever is on your mind right now. Worrying about it, trying to control it, obsessing over the details simply means that we're trying to do the job of the GPS. When we do that, we miss out on the sights all around us, the little gems in life, the joys.

Trusting the system can feel acutely difficult, especially when we've been used to trying to control everything in our lives. Letting go or simply letting it be can feel like something we're too scared to even try. A client once said that she felt like she was gripping on to a railing that was high above the ground. She was hanging on for dear life and here I was encouraging her to let go. We talked about it for a while and I asked her to look around and get an idea of the lie of the land. She began laughing as she realised that her feet were metaphorically inches above the ground. Hardly life-threatening! There's a wonderful video on YouTube of a little boy hanging onto a rope in a swimming pool. He's beside himself with terror, sobbing his little heart out. His mum encourages him to put his feet on the ground and he finds that the water barely covers the tops of his legs. Call it over-thinking, or call it our skewed relationship with thought, it's something we've all experienced in our own way.

The constant noise in our heads trying to figure stuff out, worrying about what may or may not happen in the future or fixating about something that happened yesterday, all of this drowns out our natural, innate ability to tune into and hear our inner guidance system. Learning to listen — and trust what we hear — really makes life so much easier.

We have all got so used to listening to the constant chatter, the noise, the loudness of our thinking that we assume (adding another layer of confusion) that we need to take it seriously, that because it's loud and constant, it must be important. It's not. It's just like that bossy friend who everyone goes along with because they are just loud and insistent. We don't need to take them seriously.

Think of this in relation to the eating disorder. Despite the loud voice shouting at you, urging you, befriending you, cajoling you, coercing you, somewhere deep inside (and it may be buried very deeply), there's certainty that there is another way. You might even be urged by the eating disorder to ignore that too.

When our minds become still we give our inner voice the chance to be heard. For some people it's in meditation, or yoga, or a walk on the beach. To be honest it doesn't really matter what the 'doorway' is to a quiet mind, you'll know it when you hear it. It will feel like home. Go with that feeling.

HOW DO I RECOGNISE MY INNER WISDOM?

REBECCA

"Every stressful thought separates you from your true nature." ~ Byron Katie

We've been sharing a lot about our natural state being one of wisdom, of clarity and of wellbeing. Yet we realise that perhaps this seems so far from your own truth right now. You may be feeling anything but wise or well or clear in your thoughts. Bea and I can both testify to those feelings.

"So how do I recognise this inner wisdom?" is a question you may well be asking. With so many thoughts incessantly vying for our attention it can be difficult to identify the helpful ones. Each thought seems to feel right, each is compelling in its own way, some are even mesmerising. How do we know which to take seriously and which to ignore?

Here's what I see — our wisdom is there before thought. It's our natural buoyant state of mind, again before thought. It's the clarity we have before we've 'indulged' in a lot of thinking. All our habits, personality traits and behaviours are not who we are, they are simply experiences we get to feel because we're human. We are who we are *before* our thinking gets in on the act and messes things up. This is our true nature.

For example, we might have all instinctively picked up the phone to speak to someone we've not spoken to for a long time, perhaps after we'd had a falling out, because it felt like the right thing to do, whatever the outcome. We've reached out to give someone a hug, because it felt right to do so. We've said 'no' to a request because we simply knew it was the right decision.

With wisdom there is never any doubt. There are no pros and cons to be written up; we just know. We've all experienced these moments of wisdom when we just know the right thing to do. It was my nephew's wisdom that led him to raise his concerns about Bea's health with his mum. Bea and I often found words flowed incredibly easily between us whilst writing this book — even though it's felt really tough at times, it's always felt like the right thing to do.

Our wisdom, intuition or whatever you choose to call it is gentle and full of compassion and kindness for us. Our wisdom waits for us to trust it and follow it and be guided by it. Use these positive feelings as a guide. When you have a clear mind, go with the good feeling, always.

It's important to note that wisdom isn't always the easy route. It's not necessarily pain-free. It might be that you just know without a doubt that it's time to end an unhealthy relationship; this was how I felt at the end of my marriage. It might be that wisdom is guiding you to put more on your plate although there's another voice telling you a very different story. Wisdom might be guiding you to not go to the gym again today. These might be really painful and difficult thoughts, yet you know they are right. You can feel the discomfort but somewhere inside in that quiet place, you know it's time or it's right to listen to that inner guide — your wisdom has always got your back.

In that natural good feeling state, life seems to flow, decisions are made easily and effortlessly. We are in a natural state of wellbeing. And then at some point for maybe no identifiable reason we began taking our negative thinking seriously. We took it as fact and things started to change for us. We believed things others said of us and the peaceful, perfect person we were seemed to be changing shape. We began to question everything. We began to focus more on the negative things we heard and less on the perfect knowing we once had. Does that sound familiar to you? We began to take notice of the voices we heard (our thoughts) and life became something to navigate with care and trepidation.

We became insecure and sought solace and comfort in addictions. All of this would make sense if we believe all the negativity we're hearing in our thinking.

The truth is, however, quite different. All these thoughts and feelings are experiences, they really aren't who we are. You're hearing them, but they aren't you. All thoughts and feelings are transient; they don't hang around when left alone. As I write this I'm listening to my neighbour's two-year-old having a meltdown and I know it'll be over probably by the time I get to the end of the next paragraph! Small children are so great at this. They just don't hang on to emotions. We can learn much from them about letting go.

The first step in this process is simple — just begin to notice the thinking that's running through your head. Begin to question your thinking. Notice what's being 'said', and what's really true. Practice not believing everything you think. You might find it freeing. We did and we both found it truly transformative. We know without doubt that the same is possible for you.

SECTION 6: HOPE FOR THE FUTURE

"Wellbeing is not the fruit of something you do; it's the essence of who you are. There is nothing you need to do, be, have, get, change, practice, or learn in order to be happy, loving and whole." ~ Michael Neill

Our sincerest hope is that you've found something within this book that has resonated with you. You might not even be able to put into words what it is, it might just be that you feel something differently. It's often said that it feels like nothing has changed but everything is different. Or you might simply feel confused, and that's okay too.

Rebecca heard from a client she'd recently worked with who had been struggling with an addiction. It had affected every area of his life. When they first met, he wasn't working, his partner had asked him to leave, his relationships with others wasn't good either. He told her that when he got a glimpse of how the mind really worked, when he saw the possibility of freedom, it changed everything for him. He saw for the first time in a long time that all the creative things he loved to do, photography and painting, were once again possible. There was hope, where he felt there had been none. He had in their very first conversation an inkling that life could get better. He'd been open-minded and curious enough, despite the panic he felt, to continue looking in this direction.

There is always hope.

"Never broken, nothing lacking" — these are the beautiful words Drs Bill and Linda Pettit, psychiatrist and psychologist, friends of Sydney Banks, say about each and every one of us. However broken we might feel, whatever has been said to us or of us in the past, this is not who we are. Beyond how we feel right now, whatever pain we are in we are always whole and perfect. Whatever your story seems to point towards — the self-harm, the restricting, the binge eating, the fear, the addiction, the depression, the shame — is not who you are. You are not your story. Your story is simply that... a story.

You do not need to hide from life. Nothing can break our connection to our fundamental state of being okay, to our innate mental wellbeing and resilience.

Go gently. There is ease and grace just below the surface, just beyond where you can see right now. It's there waiting to be uncovered. All you need to do is stay open and be curious as you look more in the direction in which we've been pointing.

38

THE SEARCH IS OFF

REBECCA

I had a beautiful conversation with a client recently. It feels right to share it with you here as we come towards the end of the book.

We had been speaking of the great effort involved in searching for answers, and for finding solutions. We spoke of the journeys we'd been on searching to connect with ourselves in the world out there. The times we longed for change, to stop smoking, or worrying, or start exercising, it all seemed such hard work.

- We search in the self-help section of the bookshop
- We search for a guru
- We search in online and offline courses
- We search in meditation and yoga
- We search in religion

We keep searching out there in the world and never find it. Sometimes we seem to be getting closer, sometimes we're way off. All the while it's never quite it. It's elusive. Most of the time our searching is innocently taking us further from the truth. The truth is that we're looking in the wrong places.

And what do we mean by finding ourselves anyway? What does this elusive 'it' look and feel like?

It's that place deep inside where we feel peace, calm, oneness. It's the essence of who we are. It's where anything is possible. It's a place free of judgment and self-criticism. It's a playground. It's where magic happens. And it's not out there.

This is what I see. The very thing we're out there looking for is who we are.

"You are what you seek." ~ Robert Holden

I had an insight during my conversation with a client. I saw (in fact we both saw) that the person we're striving to become truly is who we are already.

There is no "I'll be better when, I'll be happy when, I'll be successful when I've found myself". You see, we haven't gone anywhere. We are here, we always have been here. We are 'home'.

We've all simply forgotten, and over the years we got caught up in searching in the world out there.

For a while, restricting, cutting, bingeing, drinking, smoking, taking drugs, running, shopping, even yoga and meditation looks like the answer. It takes away the pain we feel when we feel lost. The times we lose touch with who we are, or don't like who we think we are, the times we are scared of the dialogue taking place in our heads, it looks helpful to numb all the noise. We are doing the best we can given the 'reality' that is taking place inside us.

When we are at our lowest ebb, when we think, "well, this must be who I really am", when we strive and struggle and work hard 'on ourselves' to find the 'real me' we are actually furthest from the truth. The map we placed such belief in is what has been taking us in the wrong direction.

Our intellect will fight with us (I'd been in that fight for many years), assuring us that this is who we really are. It's simply not true. We are, in the words of Marianne Williamson, *"powerful beyond measure"*. That's who we truly are.

So instead of it being a long and arduous journey to discover ourselves, what if it were easy? What if it were simply seeing who we really are and have been all along?

Turning inwards is always the answer. We are our own guru. The quieter we get, the less we pay attention to the thoughts in our head and the more reflective we become, the truer and clearer the answers are. With truth shining like a beacon, life would then become so different, wouldn't it? We would move from fearful to fearless. Things would go from feeling incredibly difficult to effortless. Life would be lived with love, with grace, with joy, with understanding. We could experience all of life the highs and the lows with a deeper understanding, knowing that we are all we need.

39

FALLING BACK INTO OLD BELIEFS

BEA

Since the end of 2017, I have considered myself to be fully recovered from anorexia. I always thought that it would remain a part of me. I was told that I would always have an abnormal relationship with food. So I believed that for a long time — almost eight years in fact. I now know that's not the case. Nothing about me has changed. No one has awarded me a certificate saying "Congratulations, you no longer have an eating disorder". What's changed is everything you have read about in this book.

Earlier in the book I wrote about my black list and how I no longer feel bound by it. But I felt it important to tell you that sometimes I forget. Sometimes I find myself falling back into old beliefs.

Recently, when I went out for dinner I suddenly felt totally overwhelmed by the choice on the menu. I started to slip back into the mindset of 'what should I eat' rather than 'what do I want to eat'. But after a couple of minutes I noticed where my thinking was headed so I stopped, took a few deep breaths and asked myself the question 'what do you really want to eat right now?' I looked back at the menu and chose a delicious meal.

Slipping back into this mindset isn't something that I'm ashamed of and it isn't something I beat myself up over. When you've told yourself a series of compelling stories for so long, it's unsurprising if you're unable to ditch them immediately — this is completely normal.

So when I find myself dipping back into my old habitual thinking — which I'm now getting much better at identifying — I just take a moment to remind myself that I don't need to believe those stories. I remind myself that I can eat whatever I want, whenever I want and be totally okay.

And the same applies to you. We all have our 'ifs' and 'buts' that we think make us the exception to the rule, but the bottom line is, no matter what you're thinking or believing, however compelling and real it may look, you don't have to buy into it. You can start to question and challenge your thoughts and beliefs just like I did and gradually (or sometimes quickly) you'll find that they just no longer make sense any more.

40

FREEDOM WITHIN LIFE

REBECCA

As Bea and I sit here now writing the final chapters to our book, it's truly wonderful to reflect back on just how much life has changed. I really do feel that I now have freedom in life, a real freedom to live and experience the whole of life, the ups and the downs, without fear.

It wasn't always like that. I used to be terrified of the lows and live with longing for the good moments. I felt sick a lot of the time, anticipating that things would go wrong when things were going well, and resigned to the slump when yet again I felt low. How things have changed. It's like a different life.

So, here's what I'd love to share with you now. Here are my hopes for the future given everything I've seen since coming across this understanding and given everything I now know. Here are the implications for my life and those around me both in terms of Bea's recovery and life in general.

The most important thing for me to share now is that I no

longer have any worries about Bea and anorexia. None. Before, there was always something in the back of my mind, a sense that anorexia was lying in wait for a time when life became too much for Bea and returning to restricting might look like the right thing to do. Those feelings are simply no longer there. I was actually reminded of this just yesterday evening as we sat with friends. I remembered how in the past I'd have been anxious about whether Bea would or wouldn't eat, whether she would or wouldn't join in the conversation, or whether she (or I) would or wouldn't be stressed. I smiled to myself as I realised that was then and this is now. I feel pure ease and joy knowing I no longer have to worry. My attempt at writing just how I feel simply doesn't do it justice.

Another important thing to share with you is that I no longer feel I have to be careful around Bea, biting my tongue, walking on eggshells, thinking about what I say or how I say it in case it triggers the anorexia. All this took up so much headspace and energy. As a result of this change our relationship has deepened. We've even been able to edit each other's writing without fear of upsetting each other or taking offence; this in itself speaks volumes about how much easier life is.

The impact of this understanding is not simply reserved for our dealings with the eating disorder. So much in my life has been transformed. My relationship with my partner is wonderful, our best year yet! No games, no assumptions, no second guessing what he might or might not mean by something. We both show up fully present in our relationship knowing that we love each other and we choose to be with each other every day.

I used to be a worrier and especially with my children. If I had a call with one of them and they were having a tough time I'd worry about them. I'd want to protect and 'fix' them. I'd be in touch constantly until I felt they were through their slump. Now is so different. I know that life flows through us all, the ups and the downs. I know that they, Bea and her brothers, are all okay, whatever they're going through.

It's remarkable when we see how much we've been making up in our own heads and then believing it to be real. I have so much more space to actually live life now. I don't have to work so hard and strive for happiness or peace or clarity because I know without a doubt that it's inside me. It's who I am.

41

WHOEVER, WHATEVER, WHENEVER

BEA

Before you ask, no, I'm not about to write out the lyrics to Shakira's song 'Whenever'... although for those of you who know it, it's probably now playing on loop in your head. Sorry about that.

I've been thinking about how to write this final chapter without repeating everything we've already said in our book, so I thought I'd summarise what this all means for me personally going forward in life. I have been familiar with this understanding of how the mind works for a couple of years now and, as you've read, it has had some life changing impacts. But this has extended far beyond the realm of eating disorders. For me, it feels like the boundaries and restrictions I previously constructed in my life to keep me 'safe' have faded away.

Not only do I now feel like I have fully recovered from anorexia, I am also now in a place where I am no longer crippled by the constant feelings of anxiety that I have experienced over the last few years. Much like anorexia, anxiety controlled and dictated what I could and couldn't do. Feelings of worry and panic dominated my mind for much of my waking moments. But now, without effort, those thoughts and feelings have become quiet and infrequent. They come back now and again but I no longer take them quite so seriously.

So for me, going forward, everything we've written about in this book means:

- I can be whoever I want to be and not be defined by labels or others' expectations
- I can do whatever I want and no matter what happens, I'll be okay
- I can eat whatever I want, whenever I want
- I am more confident and trust my own instincts
- I can empathise with others when they are caught in their own thinking
- I can go to a restaurant and not panic about what I can and can't eat
- I am able to notice more quickly when my thinking isn't being helpful
- I can be curious about the foods that were off limits for so long
- My mind is freed up to focus on other things
- I can enjoy food again
- I can enjoy life again.

RESOURCES

If you'd like to explore more, we've included a list of videos and books which have had an impact on us over the past couple of years. We hope they encourage you to delve a little deeper.

We're also including two beautiful poems written by friends of ours, Mary Franklin-Smith and Mahnaz Bhatti. We hope they touch you in some way as they did us.

BRAMBLE COTTAGE:

THERE'S NO SAFETY IN THORNS

By Mary Franklin-Smith

Our dear friend Mary Franklin Smith (FREED champion, Three Principles Practitioner and drama therapist at the Yorkshire Centre of Eating Disorders) who has played an important role in Bea's recovery, wrote this poem for the young women and men she treats. With her permission we share it with you here.

....And for a time I sat in a bramble bush

The deep green of the spiky leaves, my roof, walls and floor

I sat there being spiked and hurt until sit I could no more

I had heard it said, in far folk tales, that other dwellings were abound

Where instead of dark, sharp and tearing walls

Softer, lighter, kinder bricks could be found

The thing is, I know my house

It's safe in here — each room is part of me

I can find my way through corridors so very easily

I am used to being torn and poked as I wander between my chambers

And who knows what other harm might come if I were to choose different neighbours

So here I've sat, day in, day out for many days and nights

I listen to the whispering walls, I know their familiar fights

And each time that I think to poke my head out of the tunnel

I am shocked to hear the roaring waves, the windy shores that blow

And so I retreat inside my brambles to something that I know

The other day, (or was it year?)

I heard the walls in normal dispute throwing their usual jibes

And I had the thought that the voice they used was coming from somewhere inside

I had, 'til then, believed the spikes were punishment for something I'd done

But the spikes were coming not from the ground but from my own, internal tongue

As I began to speak differently to myself I noticed a most peculiar thing

... the dark green walls and thistle windows let a new shade of green and blue in

There seemed to be a different voice coming from somewhere inside

and as I listened to this softer tone, the spikes, they started to subside!

They curled up, they took a different form

and other colours began to flow

... but then I got frightened of what these new colours might show

It seemed, for a time, as I look at it now,

that I grieved the green spiky walls.

When pink, or purple or red showed up, I feared that I might fall

And so my bramble house changed this way, and that

as I choose which voice I attended

The fighting voices that scream so loud make windows that are sharp and jagged

and when I look out of these cruel frames the landscape out there is roaring

and I feel trapped inside my bramble house even though the walls are clawing

But other days the whispering voice has time to breathe and its wisdom I hear so clearly

then the windows they soften and curl and open up wide

And then something different happens inside!

And I feel a desire or is it a vision that I can live anywhere, here or down stream

And maybe my door doesn't have to be green!

And maybe my roof can be dappled with cream with clouds

and raindrops as shelter ...

It seems, to me now, as I sit here today,

that whatever the weather the wise voice doesn't go away

It's always been there waiting patiently

But for the screaming loud voices I just couldn't see

That I create my own dwelling place, my own chairs and table

When I listen to wisdom, I know I am able

And as the years have passed I have come to see

That even when I am back in Bramble cottage those spikes — they can't hurt me

Because when they sting, and sting they do

I wait for just a moment or two (and sometimes longer it's true)

But with time the dark green passes away and new colours come to play

And the less attention I give the green, the less I listen to the screams

The more I see I hold the brush — it is within me!

In fact, within each of us

I'm so pleased I know that the brambles are passing thoughts in my mind

And hurt as they do, as they try to be unkind

I breathe and I wait and soon quickly see

That the brambles are not me!

I am not my house of thorns, scratches and malice

I am the brush. I am the palette.

WISDOM IS

By Mahnaz Bhatti

Rebecca's dear friend Mahnaz wrote this at a retreat she hosted in Romania for people to explore their creativity. These are the words that came to her on the last day. With her permission we share them with you here.

Wisdom is in doing

Wisdom is the invisible Guidance which calls us to action — not because of what is on the outside but by what we are pulled to do in this moment

Wisdom is bringing the formless to form

Wisdom feels effortless

Wisdom is pure presence

Wisdom is seeing the beauty in it all

Wisdom is timeless

Wisdom is liberating

Wisdom is feeling completely connected while physically alone

Wisdom is being love while with others

Wisdom is in the silence

Wisdom plants seeds in your life in this moment from an infinite number of possibilities

Wisdom is the awareness of a new thought or idea

Wisdom is in success and in failure

Wisdom is in the words which are created from a space of not knowing

Wisdom is what the body does when you allow everything to be received and given with love

Wisdom is in being free of judgement of another, an action or a thing because it's thought which separates

Wisdom is in gratitude of it all

Wisdom is joy

Wisdom is peace

Wisdom is safe

Wisdom is forgiveness

Wisdom is an experience which you cannot realise until it has been done

Wisdom is now

Wisdom is service to our world. Our animals, our people

and our planet

Wisdom is free of control, agenda or manipulation

Wisdom is where the miracles lie

Wisdom is in the collective consciousness

Wisdom is putting pen to paper

Wisdom is dipping the brush in the paint

Wisdom is in doing nothing

Wisdom is in getting out of our own way

Wisdom is the passion which comes alive

Wisdom is standing in front of a crowd vulnerable and naked and allowing whatever comes to come

Wisdom is natural and organic

Wisdom is being connected to all that exists in this moment. Inside and out

Wisdom is courage

Wisdom is fearless

Wisdom is love

Wisdom is in doing

The rest is an illusion

The past and future

The world in which we live is a game waiting to be played. A stage on which our performance will unfold from moment to moment. A book which writes itself from moment to moment. Stories and memories which are created moment to moment. It's our personal story or experience, if you will

We are liberated

We are connected

We are whole

We are one

Live your own life to your own personal song and you will give others permission to live their lives to their own song too.

BOOKS AND VIDEOS

Books:

Bailey, Joseph. (1990) *The Serenity Principle.* Harper One.

Banks, Sydney. (reprint edition, 2016) *The Missing Link: Reflections on Philosophy and Spirit.* Lone Pine Publishing (CA)

Banks, Sydney. (reprint edition 2018) *The Enlightened Gardener.* Partners Publishing.

Bettinger, Dicken and Swerdloff, Natasha. (2016) *Coming Home: Uncovering the foundations for psychological wellbeing.* CreateSpace Independent Publishing Platform.

Brown, Brené. (2015) Daring Greatly: How the courage to be vulnerable transforms the way we live, love, parent, and lead. Penguin Life.

Dimond, Clare. (2018) *Real: The inside out guide to being yourself.* Clare Dimond

Gleason, Mara. (2017). *One Thought Changes Everything.* CreateSpace Independent Publishing Platform.

Hare, Kimberley. (2017). *The Heart of Thriving: Musings on the human experience.* Lulu Publishing Services.

Dr. Johnson, Amy. (2016). *The Little Book of Big Change: The no will-power approach to breaking any habit.* New Harbinger.

Dr. Manning, Ken, Charbit, Robin and Krot, Sandra. (2015) *Invisible Power: Insight Principles at Work.* Insight Principles, Incorporated

Neill, Michael. (2013). *The Inside Out Revolution: the only thing you need to know to change your life forever.* Hay House

Pransky, Jack. (2011). *Somebody Should Have Told Us! : Simple truths for living well.* CCB Publishing.

Videos:

The dragon story -- Michael Neill https://www.youtube.com/watch?v=7stT4OQoFGU&t=329s

Why aren't we awesomer? -- Michael Neill - https://www.youtube.com/watch?v=xr6VawX2nr4&t=9s

Mara Gleason on Confidence - https://www.youtube.com/watch?v=p04v7o_0g5A

The end of control -- Kyle Cease - https://www.youtube.com/watch?v=8tIIJgThtso&t=5s

Freedom from Binge Eating — Dr. Amy Johnson https://www.youtube.com/watch?v=tYRLhWHv3jI&t=13s

Gratitude with Louis Schwarzberg and Brother David Steindl-Rast -https://www.youtube.com/watch?v=gXDMoi-EkyuQ&t=326s

ACKNOWLEDGMENTS

We are indebted to the following people for their wisdom, love, encouragement, editing, honesty, support and reminders, some directly in conversation, some indirectly via their inspirational speaking and writing:

Mary Franklin Smith for calling out Bea's thinking on her blacklist.

Oliver Arscott, Daniel Arscott, David Arscott, Tom Baker, and Dave Graceson for your unconditional love and support. We love you.

Amy Johnson, Kimberley Hare, Mahnaz Bhatti, George and Linda Pransky, Michael Neill, Mara Olsen, Joe Bailey, Jack Pransky, Dicken Bettinger, Natasha Swerdloff, Robin Charbit, Ken Manning, and Clare Dimond for your wisdom, insights, friendship and support.

Elizabeth Baxter for being there for Bea when she needed it most.

To our editor Carol Pearson, thank you for your wonderfully sensitive work on our manuscript and for hearing our voices. And many thanks also to our star proofreaders Oliver Arscott and Sue Prosser.

And of course to Sydney Banks to whom we are grateful every day.

FIND OUT MORE:

You can find out more about us at our website Recovery from Within (http://recoveryfromwithin.life/).

We work with both families and individuals. We run workshops in London and South Wales as well as online programmes. We offer personal retreats and retreats for carers on the beautiful Gower Peninsula in South Wales.

Feel free to email anytime: hello@recoveryfromwithin.life

Follow us on Instagram:
https://www.instagram.com/recovery_from_within

Come and join our Facebook page: https://www.facebook.com/recoveryfromwithin/

59618485R00113

Made in the USA
Columbia, SC
06 June 2019